SEO

2018 SEO Handbook for Beginners

Shivani Karwal

Copyright © 2018 Shivani Karwal

Reproduction or translation of any part of this work through any means without permission of the copyright owner is unlawful and not permitted. No part of this book may be reproduced, stored in a retrieval system or transmitted by any means without permission from the copyright holder.

All rights reserved.

2018 SEO HANDBOOK FOR BEGINNERS

Learn Search Engine Optimization with Smart Strategies to Dominate Search Rankings

SHIVANI KARWAL

SEO Handbook Book Feedback:

"This book is an incredible wealth of knowledge! Some of the information was a complete eye opener for me. This book is loaded with information and is divided nicely into five books covering various aspects of digital marketing with nice lists of industry tools, FAQ sections, how-to tutorials. This book was informative and I'll be using a lot of the leanings from it for my site." ~ Amazon Customer

"Most marketing books are full of fluff, but this book is one of the most practical that I have read since I began my studies in Marketing. As a young professional, I haven't yet gotten the chance to accumulate much professional experience in digital marketing. However, this book has it all. Tips, suggestions, tool recommendations- every little technical point

you need to get your feet off the ground and become an effective digital marketer. It has all the rules and best practices to follow for SEO. Easily translatable into the professional workplace, you'll feel super confident about digital marketing strategy after reading it. 5 star rating- was worth my time and money." ~ Amazon Customer

"Great read! It was very insightful and had everything I needed to start my career in digital marketing. I highly recommend this handbook to anyone looking to increase their company's online presence or looking to enter this exciting field." ~ Amazon Customer

"We've purchased approximately ten books on this subject. This is by far the best in class. Simple, and effective!" ~ Amazon Customer

"This book is awesome! It's super easy to understand and makes digital marketing so

simple. It was the best choice I could have made. I'm new to the SEO world and I was looking for something that could help me to understand the basics. I love this book and it has given me an awesome foundation for my digital marketing career!" ~ Amazon Customer

TABLE OF CONTENTS

SEO Blueprint 3
Getting Started..4
The Three Areas of SEO...9

Site Structure

- Set up an SEO Friendly Site Structure........15
- Components of a Site Structure 15
- Do Geographic TLDS Have SEO Benefits? 16
- Subdomain vs. Subdirectory: Which is Better?..17
- Indexed vs. Non-Indexed URLs 21
- Creating SEO Friendly URLs........................22

Error Correction

- Dealing With 404s and Redirects...............23
- How to Find Errors at Scale........................26

Content

- Why is Keyword Research Important?.....28
- Detailed Steps for Conducting Keyword Research..31
- Process of Sorting Through Keywords.......37
- Different Keyword Categories....................37
- Creating a Content Plan...............................39
- How to Optimize Your Site Content...........40
- On-Page SEO Best Practices........................44
  - A. URL..44

- B. Heading Tags..........................45
- C. Image Alt Tags......................45
- D. Title Tags...............................46
- E. Meta Description..................46
- F. Keyword Density..................48

- Video Optimization Steps.........................49
- Editing and Updating Old Content............52

CTR and Rank Improvement
- How to Improve Click-Through-Rate........54
- Further Optimizing Pages About to Rank #1..56

Internal Linking
- How to Improve Click-Through-Rate........54
- How to Create a Good Internal Linking Structure for SEO...59
- Preventing Orphan Pages...........................61
- External Linking Practices..........................61

Crawlability and Indexation
- How to Create a Sitemap............................64
- How to Create a Robots.txt File.................67
- How to Get Your Pages Indexed Faster....70
- Improving Site Load Speed........................72

Off-Page SEO
- Link Building Process..................................75
- List of Link Building Ideas..........................76

- Building High Quality Links 108
- Editorial vs. Passive Links 110
- Importance of Link Anchor Text 110
- Types of Anchor Text 112
- No-follow vs. Do-follow Links 116
- The Process of Sending Outreach Emails 117
- Scaling the Outreach Process 119
- Outreach Tips 120
- Email Templates 123
- Using Search Strings for Link Prospecting 129
- Search String Examples 131
- Check Your Link Profile for Spammy Backlinks 133
- Link Earning Strategies 133
- Social Media and SEO 135

Local SEO
- Google My Business Page 139
- Citation Building 143
- Citation Format 144
- Reviews on Local Profiles 147
- On-Site Optimization for Local 149
- Keyword Research for Local SEO 150
- Building Local Links 151
- How Google Decides What to Rank 153
- Assessing Results 155

Dealing With Penalties and Algorithmic Changes

- White Hat vs. Black Hat SEO....................162
- Avoiding Penalties......................................164
- How to Check if You've Been Hit by a Penalty..164
- What to Do If Your Site Has Been Hit With a Penalty..166
- Disavow Process..167
- Reconsideration Process...........................168

SEO Checklists

- On-Page SEO..171
- Content Publishing Start to Finish..........172
- Updating Old Content...............................173
- CTR Improvement......................................174
- Further Optimizing Pages Already Ranking 175
- Keyword Research......................................176
- Video Optimization....................................177
- SEO Tasks..178
- Further Your Learning!..............................181
- Final Thoughts..185

SEO Dictionary

- Dictionary Terms..186
- Notes..252

Preface

My name is Shivani Karwal, and I'm the Founder of Digiologist - an eLearning platform providing SEO training through books and online video courses.

During my time in the industry I've come across multiple people who've told me they don't understand SEO, or it's too complicated, and I don't blame them. SEO is explained through an unnecessary filter of complexity. The internet is full of a lot of incorrect information, and it can get confusing!

My main aim while writing this book was to provide beginners with a book that leaves nothing out of the picture and makes everything as simple as possible and easy to understand. While there is a wealth of information on SEO you can find online, a lot of it is either too repetitive, not in-depth enough, too basic, outdated or simply incorrect. And to sort through it all and learn through trial and error would take a lot of your time. This book cuts through all that and will speed up SEO learning for you.

If you enjoy reading this book, please leave a review and if you want to take your learning further, check out my SEO Course at www.digiologist.com.

I hope that after reading this book, you're able to experience the power of SEO and it brings your business massive success! You can get in touch with me at shivani@digiologist.com

Thank you for reading and good luck!

Shivani Karwal

SEO Blueprint

Below is an SEO blueprint to help you visualize the different areas of SEO and what different activities fall under. This book will cover everything below and more.

Getting Started

The New Age of Marketing

Traditional mediums of marketing such as print ads, billboards, radio ads, etc. have been around since commerce existed. For most of the time since existence, marketing has been offline and through mediums such as posters, billboards, print ads in newspapers or magazines, radio, etc. These mediums still prevail, but come the late 1990s, the internet came into existence and online became a whole new medium to market through. SEO, PPC, Content Marketing, social media were all in the early phases of development at that time.

Come present day and various elements of digital marketing are in full play and it's more important than ever for your business to have a strong online presence. The Internet is accessible to almost anyone and you need to take advantage of that!

So don't just concentrate on the traditional offline methods but explore the massive online world for your marketing efforts. There are over 3 billion Internet users worldwide, and more than 70% of them use it daily, resulting in over 3.5 billion daily searches on Google! If your business isn't online, think of all the possible customers you're losing out on and all the money you're not making! Your business could make 10, 20, 30… who knows how many times more money with a stronger digital presence!

What is Online Marketing?

Online marketing a.k.a. digital marketing or internet marketing, is simply marketing through the internet, involving using the web to promote a product or service. It mainly uses electronic devices such as PCs, laptops, phones, and tablets to promote the message through online connectivity.

All this can be done in many ways such as:

1. Search Engine Optimization
2. Pay Per Click Marketing
3. Content Marketing
4. Social Media Marketing
5. Email Marketing

Search Engine Optimization

For a brief introduction before we dive into details, SEO is the process of getting a site to rank well organically in search engines to receive maximum impressions and click-throughs from users searching queries related to your site. Ideally, you want to rank your site on the first page while aiming for the top 3 positions with ranking at the first position being your ultimate goal. Did you know that the first position gets 33% of the search traffic? The second position receives an average of 18% with the click-throughs declining for the remaining positions. So only ranking alone won't cut it. You could be ranking on pages in the search results where no one sees you. So it's important to get your site pages to rank in the top positions for maximum click-throughs.

For setting everything up, the first thing you need to do is choose a domain name for your website. Some business owners underestimate the importance of having a website and skip having one. If you don't have a site, you're losing possible business. Did you know more than 3.5 billion searches are conducted on Google each day? Everything is moving online now so having a strong digital presence is key. A large number of searches are being conducted online, and a part of them are for your industry! If you don't have a website, you don't even have a chance of ranking for those search queries and have possible customers find you.

Get started by choosing a good domain name. As a business owner, the best domain name option would be to go with your brand name for relevancy and brand positioning purposes. It doesn't need to be an exact match to the keyword you're trying to rank for. Although it helps to an extent and used to be an old tactic for ranking, it's not mandatory and ends up looking unprofessional. Most sites that rank are branded non-keyword names anyway.

Three Areas of SEO

Before we dive into the details of each, let's briefly discuss the different parts of SEO first. SEO efforts can mainly be categorized into three sections:

1. On-page SEO
2. Off-page SEO
3. Local SEO

For quick differentiation between the three, on-page SEO deals with everything you do on your site, off-page SEO deals with what is done on external sites, and local SEO includes both on-site and off-site efforts done to increase rankings in local search results and for localized keywords.

On-page SEO

On-page SEO involves making efforts on the actual site itself in the following areas:

1. Having a good site structure
2. Removal of errors such as 404s, duplicate content, etc.
3. Targeting relevant keywords on your pages by publishing new content
4. Updating, improving and further optimizing old content
5. Improving click through rates
6. Creating a good internal linking structure
7. Ensuring your site is easy to crawl and pages are indexed

Some of the on-page elements that need to be optimized are the title tags, meta descriptions, headers, page content, image alt text. This is done by placing keywords you want to rank for in the content of these elements. All of this is explained in more detail later on. It also involves having a good site structure that is clean and easy for the search engine crawlers to read and index as well as for the user to navigate. You also need to create an internal linking structure wherein you cross-link your pages using relevant anchor text and frequently link to the top and important pages from your secondary pages. You also need to ensure your site is always error-free without any broken links, incorrect redirects, no duplicate content, etc.

Because on-page takes place on your site, it's all in your control, and that makes it easier. And since it's within one's control, most sites have their on-page SEO going strong, so relying on on-page techniques alone won't fully help you achieve top ranks.

Off-page SEO

Off-page SEO is a bit more difficult as it requires more time and takes place on external sites, so the control factor is lower.

Off-page SEO mainly involves efforts in three areas:

1. Building incoming links from external sites pointing to your site
2. Link earning
3. Getting social shares of your site content

Even though social shares are a not a significant part of SEO, signals such as your content being shared socially are valuable to search engines and seen as indicators of good content. Off-page SEO gives search engines an indication of how your site is doing compared to others and each link pointing to your site and social share of your content is viewed as a vote of approval from others. And the more of them you get, the better it is for your ranking. Of course, a variety of factors matter like the quality and relevancy of the sites linking to you, which will be discussed later on.

Local SEO

Local SEO is essential for businesses with a physical address and those targeting a particular geographical region. If your business has a physical location, local SEO can help you:

1. Rank for location-based keywords
2. Rank in search results for searches being conducted near and in your location and make you visible to searchers in your area
3. Rank better in the local versions of search engines

You must have already come across local search results before while searching for a product or service and having the results come up with a map known as the local pack or in the sidebar in the knowledge graph.

Site Structure

Ensuring Your Site Structure is SEO Friendly

Getting your site structure correct is very important. The way your site is laid out and content is organized, stored and presented affects not only your sites user-friendly ability but also the ability of search engines to be able to find and crawl your site. A clean and well laid out site structure is easier for search engines to find and read and improves your crawl rate, thus increasing your chances of ranking.

Components of a Website Structure

1. TLD: The top-level domain is the part of the site address that comes after the dot like .com, .net, .org, .gov, .edu, etc.

2. SLD: The second level domain is the domain name itself and the part of the site address located to the left of the dot.
3. Subdomain: The subdomain, which is also known as the third level domain, is the part before the SLD and takes the format www.subdomain.domain.com
4. Subdirectory: The subdirectory is the part after the slash after .com and takes the format www.domain.com/subdirectory

Do Geographic TLDS Have SEO Benefits?

Most people go with .com but if you're targeting a specific geographical area only, go with the one designed for your country. For example, if you're located in Canada and only do business in Canada, choose a .ca. Country-specific TLDs are known to rank better in local search results and the local versions of search engines, so they're highly beneficial for location-specific businesses. If you have multiple locations, you can even fit the ccTLD as a subdirectory like www.site.com/ca.

Some other examples of TLDs:

.com: Stands for 'commercial' and can be used by anyone in general
.org: Used by non-profit organizations
.co: Stands for 'company'
.edu: For educational sites
.gov: For government sites

Subdomain vs. Subdirectory

One of the things you may need to set up and choose between is either a subdomain or subdirectory if you require them. You'll need this for setting up the blog section of your site. More on the benefits of business blogging is in the content marketing section.

Subdomains and subdirectories are used for creating specific areas on your site for particular content. They're great for sectioning off parts of your site topic wise. But which of the two is better?

Subdirectories are the more popular choice and what I use on my site personally. Google considers a subdomain a completely separate domain. So if you're using a subdomain, you're diluting the value of your site between your domain and subdomain. A subdomain is treated as a separate site, so it doesn't receive any of the authority or positive signals such as backlinks from your main site. This makes ranking a subdomain tougher as well. A subdirectory, on the other hand, is considered a part of your domain and a much better choice as it's able to take advantage of your main domains already built up authority.

Do TLDs Affect Rankings?

Any TLD can rank in search engines whether it's an old and commonly used TLD or a new one, as long as the TLD you've chosen is relevant and applicable. The reason why we don't see many uncommon TLDs rank such as .lawyer or .travel etc. is that not many people are using them yet. Because they're not used as widely as .com, people tend to believe they're harder to rank but that's not true. But at the same time, they don't have any added advantages either. They're only good for relevancy purposes. As far as credibility goes, uncommon TLDs can appear untrustworthy to some as they're unknown and haven't made their mark yet. So if possible, stick to getting a .com.

Make sure your site is not invisible to search engines. A site can become invisible to search engines if the site structure is not readable by site crawlers. You can prevent that from happening by:

- Creating more links on your site by interlinking your pages.
- Creating a sitemap and uploading to Google webmasters.
- Creating a sitemap for your readers that is publicly displayed on your actual site. This one refers to the one created for users, which is different from the one you create for web crawlers

You can find out if your site is being crawled and indexed by search engines by doing a quick search. Open google.com and type in: site:domain.com

Google will then come back with results for the above search query and show the pages indexed. If you find a low ratio of pages indexed vs. your existing number of pages, create a sitemap and submit it to Search Console or re-submit your existing sitemap to have the crawl rate increased initially.

You can submit your site or the URL of a new page to Google in your Search Console account at https://www.google.com/webmasters/tools/submit-url

Indexed vs. Non-Indexed URLs

Not all of the pages on your site will be indexed as Google can't get to all of them with the millions of sites out there it has to get to. Some of the pages not indexed by Google are intentionally left out at times such as blog category pages, author pages,

404 error pages, pages with duplicate content, pages blocked by robots.txt, etc.

Creating SEO Friendly URLs

- Contain a keyword so you can target search traffic for that keyword.
- Not very lengthy (try to stay at under 80 characters for the entire link)
- Not deeply sub-foldered down. Try staying a maximum of 3 sub-folders down as deeper pages are crawled at a lower rate.
- Keep your URLs descriptive so don't use a number or random character strings.
- You don't need to include stop words. They're unnecessary and only lead to increasing the URL length.

Error Correction

Dealing With Errors and Redirects: 404s, 301s, and 302s

404 Not found error pages a.k.a. broken links will occur if you remove a lot of pages and don't redirect them elsewhere. For example, if you have a lot of blog posts from the past and some of the content is outdated and you remove the pages without redirecting them, the pages will then no longer have the content, but the URLs of the pages which once existed will have links pointing to them from other sites. You will have people clicking on those links, only to end up opening a 404 not found error page on your site.

The two redirects you can use are:

301: A permanent redirect

302: A temporary redirect

So if you're deleting content, make sure to redirect to either:

1. The old link either to the new page where the new content is
2. The new URL in case you're keeping the content but just updating the URL
3. The most relevant page or the homepage

In the cases where the content of a page has permanently moved to another page, or you just want a page to permanently redirect to another page with similar content, use a 301 redirect, which is a permanent redirect.

A 302 redirect, which is a temporary redirect can be used if the page you want to redirect to is under construction or if you want all clicks to the page under temporary construction to point to another page instead while it's being built.

404s are something all sites have from time to time so don't worry too much about them but keep fixing them periodically. Having too many 404 error pages will lead to more bounces and more visitors turning away from your site if they can't find what they're looking for. You can easily find your 404s in Google Search Console and create redirects using the Yoast SEO plugin.

A good practice is to create a custom 404 page so in case of unavoidable error pages coming up for visitors when they misspell links or enter in pages that don't exist; they're presented with a custom 404 page giving them options to check out other pages.

Finding Errors at Scale

There's no need to manually find errors like 404s or anything you're missing like page titles, meta descriptions, alt tags, etc. You can find them at scale using a tool like SEMrush. Run a site audit through it and it will come back with a list of everything you're missing, current errors and improvement opportunities like below:

You can set up multiple audits like below to check errors in various areas like on-page, spammy backlinks, etc. and have them emailed to you so, you're always in the loop.

SEO Handbook

Site Audit 10h ago Health score **40%** -2%	**Position Tracking** The Position Tracking Tool allows you to get daily updates on positions in Google's top 100 organic and paid search results. 🔧 Set up	**On Page SEO Checker** On Page SEO Checker offers a complete and structured list of things you can do to improve the search engine optimization for select pages of your website. 🔧 Set up About
Pages with issues **3,662** Out of 4,382 checked pages		
Social Media Tracker Social Media Tracker will let you track social audience, activity and engagement of you and your competitors in Facebook, Twitter, Google+, Instagram and YouTube. 🔧 Set up	**Social Media Poster** Publish and schedule posts across major social networks, save time on social managing, analyze your content performance and more! 🔧 Set up	**Brand Monitoring** The Brand Monitoring tool allows you to easily track all mentions of your and your competitors' brand, product or service on the web and social media. 🔧 Set up About
Backlink Audit Toxic domains **220** Referring Domains **676**	**Link Building** Prospects **564**	**PPC Keyword Tool** Search, create and manage your keywords with the SEMrush PPC Keyword tool. Create different campaigns and ad groups with just one click. 🔧 Set up
Ad Builder Ad Builder helps you create compelling ad texts. Analyze your competitors' ads, preview your ads and assign the newly created ads to existing keyword groups. 🔧 Set up	**Organic Traffic Insights** Connect your GA and GSC accounts to unlock 'not provided' keywords and see the actual organic traffic driven by them. 🔧 Set up	**Content Analyzer** Audit your domain content and track your guest posts to pinpoint high-exposure content. 🔧 Set up

Content

Why Keyword Research is Important

Keyword research is important because it helps target keywords of value. If you blindly optimize for keywords without research, you:

1. You might end up trying to rank for keywords with high competition, only to not be able to rank for them at all, resulting in lost time and wasted effort.
2. You might end up targeting keywords with low search volume and end up receiving little to no traffic that wasn't worth the time to target it

Keyword research is the first and most important step of optimization. All your optimization efforts are based on the keywords you choose to target, so they need to be chosen with much thought and numbers to back your decision.

Keyword research doesn't involve just choosing a bunch of keywords relevant to you and stuffing your site pages with them. Yes, relevance is important, but numbers are important too. You need to look into how much traffic those keywords are getting and how tough it will be to rank for them.

There are keywords that are relevant and have high search volumes but are also very competitive to rank for so going after them may not always result in anything. Depending on your site authority, it may be better to put your effort into targeting keywords that are less competitive as it's better to rank well for a keyword with lower search volume than to not rank at all for a keyword with higher search volume.

Some things you should ask yourself while choosing your keywords:

1. Are the keywords you're choosing being searched enough times for you to get decent traffic from them if you rank?
2. Are the keywords you're choosing easy to rank for keeping in mind your current site authority?
3. Do the keywords have enough traffic from locations your product or service is sold in?
4. Are the keywords relevant to your site?

Steps for Conducting Keyword Research

You can find relevant keywords using any of the numerous keyword research tools. The ones I use are SEMRush and Keywordtool.io. They will give you a massive list of keywords and their competitiveness levels and search volume, allowing you to narrow down to the ones best suited to your site.

Here's an outline of the steps to take while conducting keyword research:

Brainstorm a list of all possible keywords and keyphrases you can think of. You can do this a few ways. Make an entire list of keywords that are relevant to your business that people might be putting into search engines to find businesses like yours. Stretch those keywords into key phrases and make a list of those too. Come up with different ways of saying the same thing (use synonyms) and expand your list. You should roughly have around 10-15 terms to start with.

For example, if you have a luxury jewelry store, just some of the examples of keywords that immediately come to mind are:

- gold jewelry
- platinum jewelry
- silver jewelry
- diamond jewelry

These are just the main basic keywords. You can add more detail and also add location modifiers for wherever your store is located and get 'gold jewelry store Toronto' and so on. You can also add queries for additional services you offer or things you think people might be looking for such as 'jewelry repair', 'ring cleaning' etc.

Once you have 5-10 of your main broad keywords, input them one at a time in your keyword research tool of choice, and it will come back with thousands of keywords based on your input. There's no need for guesswork here or to come up with keywords on your own as the tool does everything for you, coming back with results based on actual keyphrases being searched by users.

For example, if I input one of the above keywords such as 'silver jewelry' into SEMRush to start with, it comes back with 2,000+ keywords!

PHRASE MATCH KEYWORDS (2,091)

Keyword	Volume	CPC (USD)	SERP
silver jewelry	5,400	2.13	
sterling silver jewelry	3,600	2.34	
how to clean silver jewelry	3,600	0.33	
silver jewelry cleaner	2,400	0.66	
sterling silver cremation jewelry	1,600	1.65	

You can also look into the related keywords report to uncover many more ideas you might not have considered that don't contain exact matches of your seed keywords. Keywords related to 'silver jewelry' bring back another 1,400+ keywords:

RELATED KEYWORDS REPORT 1 - 100 (1,498)

Keyword	Related %	Volume
silver jewlry	80.00	140
silver jewerly	75.00	2,400
silver and jewelry	75.00	30
silver jewdrey	75.00	20
sterling silver jewelry	70.00	3,600
sterling silver jewlry	70.00	50
sterling silver jewlery	65.00	1,900
sterling silver jewerly	65.00	210
sterling silver store	65.00	210
silver jewerly store	65.00	140
sterling silver jewelery	65.00	90
silver jewelry for sale	65.00	40

After inputting 5-10 of your main broad keywords, you'll have a massive list of thousands of keywords, part of which will look like:

	A	B	C
1	Keyword	Search Volume	Keyword Difficulty Index
2	silver jewelry	5400	81.39
3	sterling silver jewelry	3600	81.41
4	how to clean silver jewelry	3600	87.19
5	silver jewelry cleaner	2400	83.43
6	sterling silver cremation jewelry	1600	64.5
7	wholesale sterling silver jewelry	880	52.85
8	silver spoon jewelry	880	77.61
9	silver and turquoise jewelry	720	71.54
10	mens silver jewelry	720	74.97
11	silver indian jewelry	720	63.74
12	how to clean sterling silver jewelry	720	87.46
13	cremation jewelry sterling silver	720	63.73
14	wholesale silver jewelry	720	52.13
15	antique silver jewelry box	720	80.1
16	silver forest jewelry	720	74.14
17	silver mountain jewelry	590	80.03
18	how to clean silver jewelry at home	590	91.12
19	clean silver jewelry	590	88.64
20	sterling silver jewelry cleaner	590	87.5
21	silver jewelry osrs	590	68.42
22	cheap sterling silver jewelry	590	81.63
23	silver jewelry box	590	88.94
24	mens sterling silver jewelry	480	71.86

Your list can turn out to be upwards of 10K keywords but don't get scared due to the size. Once you have the list, you're going to filter through it to sort and narrow it down to your main targets.

You can sort your keyword list based on:

1. Search volume
2. Competitiveness levels

Choose the golden opportunities, i.e., keywords that have the combination of high search volume and low ranking competition. These keywords are the ones that will be easier to rank for and have enough search traffic, so they're worth putting in the effort for.

Another way you can find keyword opportunities is by checking what keywords your competitors rank for. You can input their website into a rank checker tool to get all the data. This will help uncover some good finds.

Process of Sorting Through Keywords

You can then further sort your keyword list into the following categories:

1. **Primary Keywords:** The main service or product related keyword(s) you want to rank for that will bring you the most business. This is usually one or two keywords only. This is the keyword you'll be inputting into the home-page as it has the most authority and ranking power.
2. **Secondary Keywords:** These are other service or product related keywords but have slightly less search volume as compared to the primary keyword. These are usually less than 10 in number and are targeted through pages as well in the form of evergreen content.

3. **Service or Product Related Keywords:** These are all remaining service or product based keywords other than the primary and secondary keywords. Service and product based keywords are important because due to the search intent with the buyer being in the final stages of the buyer's cycle, i.e., ready to purchase, they bring in traffic resulting in actual conversions instead of just casual traffic looking only to read a blog post.

4. **Location Modifier Keywords:** If you run a location-specific business, ranking for location-specific keywords is important so you can attract targeted search traffic instead of targeting general visitors from locations you don't even service.

5. **Longtail Keywords:** Longtail keywords are key phrases that are more than four words in length. These mostly have lower search

volume but are also usually easier to rank for so make good low hanging fruit.
6. **Question Keywords:** These are longtail keywords as well but can be looked into as a separate category as not all longtail keywords are questions. These are good for blog posts, for an ask the experts section or a FAQs section.
7. **Evergreen Content Keywords:** You can target important keywords with lengthier evergreen content created to rank long-term
8. **Blog Post Keywords:** These can be targeted through shorter blog posts.

Creating a Content Plan

Once you have your final keyword list ready, you can create a content plan based on the keyword categories sorted by highest search traffic levels. I usually do this in Google Sheets and create columns for the keyword, content type, article title, word count, etc. Since you're already knowledgeable of your niche, you can create engaging and valuable thought leadership style content. When others see you as being knowledgeable about your niche and producing valuable content, they can trust you a lot more. Make your content so good that they want to buy from you without a thought.

	A	B	C	D	E
1	Content Plan:				
2	Keyword	Search Volume	Competition	Type	Content Title
3	silver vs gold jewelry	170	80.22	Evergreen	Silver vs. Gold Jewelry: Which Should You Wear?
4	silver jewelry canada	50	52.54	Location	Shop Silver Jewelry in Canada
5	sterling silver jewelry	2400	83.43	Product	Buy Sterling Silver Jewelry Online
6	how to clean sterling silver jewelry	720	87.46	Longtail	How to Clean Sterling Silver Jewelry
7	silver jewelry	5400	81.39	Primary	Buy Silver Jewelry - Shop Online

How to Optimize Your Site Content

Once you have your list of targeted keywords, you can add them to your pages in the following areas:

- Title tag
- Meta description
- Article title/Page Title
- Heading tags
- In the content body
- URL of the page
- Description and alt text of the images

You can easily add keywords into the above fields in your content management system like WordPress and by using an on-page SEO plugin like Yoast:

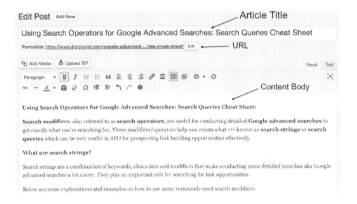

The previous screenshot shows you the different fields where you can input your article title, URL and content.

The screenshot below is what shoes up when you upload an image, allowing you to add your image alt text.

URL	https://www.digiologist.com/
Title	google advanced search
Caption	
Alt Text	google-advanced-search
Description	Search operators to conduct a Google advanced search.

Below is a screenshot of the Yoast SEO plugin which allows you to add your title tag and meta description:

Once you're done optimizing, based on the keyword you put in the focus keyword bar, the Yoast SEO plugin will give you a list of improvements to make:

Analysis

Problems (2)
- The keyword density is 0.2%, which is too low; the focus keyword was found 3 times.
- A meta description has been specified, but it does not contain the focus keyword.

Improvements (3)
- The images on this page do not have alt attributes containing the focus keyword.
- The SEO title contains the focus keyword, but it does not appear at the beginning; try and move it to the beginning.
- The slug for this page is a bit long, consider shortening it.

Good (8)
- The focus keyword appears in the first paragraph of the copy.
- The meta description has a nice length.
- The text contains 1814 words. This is more than or equal to the recommended minimum of 300 words.
- This page has 0 nofollowed outbound link(s) and 5 normal outbound link(s).
- This page has 0 nofollowed internal link(s) and 1 normal internal link(s).
- The SEO title has a nice length.
- The focus keyword appears in the URL for this page.
- You've never used this focus keyword before, very good.

On-Page SEO Best Practices:

URL:

- Contains the targeted keyword
- Words are separated by hyphens

- No need to include stop words
- The entire URL including the domain and subfolders is less than 100 characters

Heading Tags H1 - H6:

- You don't need to use all six tags. Only if you have six headings
- Don't use the same text for the content title and H1 as it looks unnatural. You can, however, keep the title tag and H1 the same as the title tag only appears in SERPs.

Image Alt Tag and Description:

- The image alt tag or alt text should be roughly a max of 5-6 words and under 80 characters.
- Should be descriptive to the image
- Should have the words separated by hyphens

Title Tag:

- You can add your company name at the end with a vertical | separator to increase brand recognition and click-throughs
- Should be under 60 characters for it to fully display in the SERPs. Otherwise, it will get cut off.

Note that the page/article title and title tag are both different. They're both titles for the page but the title tag is shown as the title in search results, and the page/article title is shown as the title on your site. You can keep them both the same or slightly change them as well but be sure to use the character limit available.

Meta Description:

- Should be under 160 characters for it to fully display. Otherwise, it will get cut off in the search results.

Meta description is important as it increases click-through rate in the SERPs if the keyword the user is searching for is in the meta description as well but adding your targeted keywords into meta description does not affect ranks.

The title tag will appear at the top of your listing in the search engine results as the heading, and the meta description will appear under it as the description. The title tag, meta description, and URL are what users see when they view your site listed in search engines and based on that they decide whether to click on your site or not, so all 3 of these are very important for achieving good CTRs. Make them unique, informative, useful, relevant, interesting and captivating enough to receive the maximum click-through rates.

Keyword Density

- Should be between 1-3%. Anything more than that would be considered keyword stuffing.

In addition to the above, it is important to keep in mind the keyword density of the content and to try to place the keyword at the beginning, within the first 100 words at least. The keyword density is the percentage of the number of times the keyword appears in the body of the content based on the total number of words in the content. Try keeping the density between 2% to 3% and try to make this look as natural as possible so don't repeat your keyword too many times. You don't need to calculate this percentage manually. Your SEO plugin will do that for you.

It's important to write the content for your reader first and foremost and secondly for search engine ranking purposes. If you add your keyword too many times in your content for ranking purposes, your content is going to end up not being very useful to the reader, and they will shut your page immediately, thus spending less time on your site, which Google takes as your page not being helpful and lowers your rankings. So keyword stuffing will ultimately backfire on you.

I didn't include meta tags in the above list as Google no longer considers them. They're still used by search engines like Yahoo and Bing though, but since the bulk of organic search traffic comes from Google, you can overlook adding them.

Optimization Process for Videos

This book mainly covers optimizing content in the form of text and images, but I want to go over video optimization as well. Video content is huge!

With YouTube being the second largest search engine after Google, you can't skip video content creation. While uploading videos on YouTube, the optimization process is similar to on-page SEO for articles wherein you're simply targeting keywords by placing them in various areas, with just the areas being slightly different for the two. Below is a list of places where you need to add your keywords to your video as well as a few other things to do:

1. Look up keywords for your video using a YouTube keyword tool such as Keywordtool.io and input your keywords into the following:
- Video title: Add the keyword towards the beginning of the title.
- Video description: Add the main keyword a few times for good keyword density and add in your secondary keywords as well.

- Tags: Add your main keyword as well as all related keywords into the tags. Fill this to the max keywords you can fit in.
- Video thumbnail file image
- Video file name

2. Timestamps: Create a video timeline using timestamps. These are easy to create and all you need to do is make a list of the main topics you discuss in your video and list them in the description with the exact minute and second timeline mark they're started at in the video. That will allow you to add the mini topic names in your description, thus resulting in targeting more keywords.

3. Closed captions and transcripts: This isn't necessary so you can skip adding these as they're time-consuming but if you can, you can add closed captions or transcripts. It will allow you to add more text to your videos, resulting in keywords being picked up by YouTube.

4. Add your videos to relevant playlists with each playlist having an SEO friendly title and description.
5. Interlink your videos to each other through cards and video displays at the end.

Editing and Updating Old Content

It's a good practice to update and improve previously written content. That helps improve the content and make it better as well as update it per the latest information in your industry. Editing previous content is seen as a good sign by Google and helps keep your content fresh and prevents it from being buried and hidden once it gets old.

To successfully edit your content:

1. Update it to follow the latest information on that topic
2. Add more text to lengthen your content

3. Add in images if missing or add more
4. Embed in a video, infographic or other media like a podcast, etc
5. Add in a call to action if this is something you weren't doing before
6. Re-optimize it for a better keyword if there is one or further optimize it for the current keyword if you missed out on some optimization opportunities

CTR Improvement and Improving Ranks

Click-Through-Rate Improvement

CTR improvement i.e. click-through-rate improvement results in making more people click on your results in search engines.

In Google Search Console under search analytics, you can find your sites impressions in search and the resulting click-throughs. Impressions are how many times your site is viewed by users in search results for various keywords, and click-throughs are how many clicks took place as a result of those impressions. In Search Console, you'll notice your impressions will be a lot higher than clicks, and that's normal.

The idea here is to increase the click-throughs for impressions you're already getting. Half the work is already done here as your site is receiving those views in SERPs. You need to leverage that and increase clicks for impressions you're already receiving.

One of the main reasons why those impressions are not converting to clicks is a boring (or even missing) title tag and meta description. So find all of your missing title tags and meta descriptions and fill them in and improve the existing ones to make them more clickable. All of these changes will be made for specific keywords as you can look into exactly which keywords the pages are getting impressions for and then optimize them further for those keywords.

This helps in achieving two things: not only do you end up making your title tag and meta description more relevant around that keyword and receive more clicks, but you also end up further optimizing your page for that keyword if you weren't already, thereby ranking higher and receiving more impressions.

Further Optimizing Pages About to Rank

It's a lot easier to increase the rank of a page already ranking than to rank one from scratch. Your site has many pages that are ranking, but some of them are not ranking well and you need to bump them up.

In your rank checker tool, check which keywords are closer to ranking #1, i.e., keywords that are ranking positions 2 - 20.

Download the list of those keywords (along with which URLs are ranking for those keywords, which is something the tool will pull for you).

Remove the keywords with lower search monthly volume (like less than 100) that aren't worth putting the time in to rank for.

Then, for the list of remaining keywords, build backlinks for the URLs ranking, using the keywords as anchor text. Build these backlinks as an internal link from within your site as well as one external link. The reason I say one external link is because we're using the exact match of the keywords as anchor text so we don't want to overuse it and get penalized.

The external site you build the link on can be anywhere that's high quality and will result in a do-follow link such as a social bookmarking site, a web 2.0 site, etc. You can create the link using Google Sites which is safe and something you'll never get penalized for as it's a Google product. You can also create it on web 2.0 sites like Blogspot or WordPress (the .com version which is free). The idea here is to create the links fast with minimal effort and without any site authority taking them down.

Internal Linking

Importance:

- Help users navigate your content better
- Allow you to link out to relevant content
- Help search engine crawlers find your pages faster
- Allow you to choose the anchor text and link placement of your choice

Creating and Following a Good Internal Linking Structure

- Each page on the site has at least one internal link pointing to it
- Anchor texts for the internal links and keyword rich
- Internal links are not no-follow

- A majority of your pages link to the sites main pages like the home page and important pages like services, about us, etc
- The homepage links to folder level 2 pages, level 2 pages link to level 3 pages and the same from bottom to top.
- Don't forget to link to your deeper pages as they're the pages the crawlers are less likely to reach.

Make it a practice to do the following each time you publish a new piece of content:

1. Add an internal link in the article pointing to another page o your site
2. Add an internal link on another page linking to the new piece of content

Preventing Orphan Pages

Orphan pages are pages that are not linked to from other pages on your site. They're pages on your site with no internal links pointing to them. Orpha pages are not something we want, so it's a good idea to ensure every page on your site has at least one internal link pointing to it. One way you can ensure that is to make it a habit to add an internal link to your content as soon as you publish it.

External Linking Practices

External links are all outgoing links you post on your site linking to other sites. It's a good idea to add outgoing links to external pages that are relevant to the content you're posting. Make sure the outgoing links are relevant and not to spammy sites. You can make it a practice to link to 1-2 outgoing links in your articles if required but try not to add more as it will devalue the link power to your internal links on that page as link juice will be split across all links on the page.

Crawlability and Indexation

Once you have your site up and running, some of the first few things you'll need to set up are:

1. Sitemap (both for the user and search engines)
2. Robots.txt

And of course, if you haven't already, it's highly recommended you create accounts for your site on Google Analytics and Search Console (formerly known as Google Webmaster Tools). Google Analytics will keep track of all incoming traffic and its sources and Search Console will help in keeping you up to date on any problems occurring on your site.

Creating a Sitemap

This sitemap is like the layout for your site and shows all of the pages and their hierarchy. It makes it a lot easier for search engines to crawl your website and for users to navigate your site. But note that there are two separate sitemaps: one for search engines and one for the user.

The sitemap for search engines is called an XML sitemap and is automatically created using the Yoast SEO plugin for WordPress. If you're not using Yoast, I highly recommend you do so as it's handy for on-page SEO and makes keyword targeting very easy. If you already use Yoast, it probably already has the sitemap created for you on your site on the page located at .com/sitemap_index.xml

A sitemap is important as it helps search crawlers:

1. Crawl your site faster
2. Know the priority of pages while crawling them
3. Tells them when the pages were last updated/edited and how frequently

Once you locate your sitemap, upload it to Google Search Console, formerly known as Google Webmasters Tools. If you're not using WordPress, you can always manually create your sitemap using a sitemap creator such as xml-sitemaps.com. Then download the file and upload it to Search Console.

You upload your sitemap in Search Console by clicking Crawl > Sitemaps > Add/Test Sitemap in the left-hand sidebar.

Click 'add a sitemap' and upload the file. If you do not have a Google Webmasters Tools account yet, get one by signing up at google.com/webmasters.

https://www.digiologist.com/sitemap_index.xml

XML Sitemap

Generated by **YoastSEO**, this is an XML Sitemap, meant for consumption by search engines.

You can find more information about XML sitemaps on **sitemaps.org**.

This XML Sitemap Index file contains 9 sitemaps.

Sitemap	Last Modified
https://www.digiologist.com/post-sitemap.xml	2018-03-25 22:49 +00:00
https://www.digiologist.com/page-sitemap.xml	2017-12-08 15:41 +00:00
https://www.digiologist.com/course-sitemap.xml	2016-10-01 04:15 +00:00
https://www.digiologist.com/unit-sitemap.xml	2015-07-11 03:26 +00:00
https://www.digiologist.com/product-sitemap.xml	2017-12-08 07:43 +00:00
https://www.digiologist.com/category-sitemap.xml	2018-03-25 22:49 +00:00
https://www.digiologist.com/post_tag-sitemap.xml	2017-01-20 17:36 +00:00
https://www.digiologist.com/course-cat-sitemap.xml	2016-10-01 04:15 +00:00
https://www.digiologist.com/module-tag-sitemap.xml	2016-03-19 23:23 +00:00

Creating a Robots.txt File

A robots.txt file instructs search engine crawlers which page to skip crawling and not include in search results. These are pages you don't want to be shown in search results such as login pages, member areas, etc.

Some examples of cases where a robots.txt files can be used:

1. To block images from being crawled in the case of the site owner not wanting them to rank in search engines
2. To tell search engines to ignore duplicate content on your site
3. To prevent search engines from accessing certain areas of your site you don't want to rank such as old outdated content.

4. To prevent certain pages from ranking such as the user login area, admin panel, member areas, etc.
5. To prevent your entire website from being crawled and shown in results

To create a robots.txt file script to prevent certain areas of your site from ranking in search results, follow the format below:

User-agent: *
Disallow: /example/

In place of example, type in the page you don't want to be crawled. For example, if you want your member login area page located at site.com/member-login to be blocked from crawlers, your file would contain the following:

User-agent: *

Disallow: /member-login

You can copy your script and upload it to Yoast SEO in the file editor section. If you're not using WordPress, you can create the above file and save it as a word document and upload it to the root directory of your website.

robots.txt Tester

Edit your robots.txt and check for errors. Learn more.

Latest version seen on 3/21/18, 7:02 AM OK (200) 187 Bytes

```
1  User-agent: *
2  Disallow: /wp-admin/
3
4
```

0 Errors 0 Warnings

The robots.txt file needs to be created with extreme care. Even a slight mistake can end up excluding all or many of your pages from being indexed and preventing you from ranking in search engines, resulting in lost traffic. If you don't have any pages to block from search engines, skip creating a robots.txt file because you don't need it.

```
User-agent: *
Allow: /
```

How to Get Your Site and New Pages Indexed Faster

You can always sit back and wait for Google to index your site but there are ways to make it happen faster, allowing you to take advantage of potential organic traffic now instead of later. Below are some tips on getting your site indexed by Google more quickly:

1. **Sitemap:** Create and upload an XML sitemap in Search Console so Google can crawl your pages faster.
2. **Internal Links:** Follow a good internal linking structure on your site where each page links to at least one internal page on your site, internal links use good anchors, link up to the main pages on your site and create internal links to newly published pages on your site.
3. **External Links:** Backlinks help Google reach your site as well so follow link building strategies to gain links.
4. **Submit to Google:** In addition to submitting your sitemap to Google, you can also submit your URLs manually as well to:

https://www.google.com/webmasters/tools/submit-url

5. **Fetch as Google:** In Search Console, click on Crawl > Fetch as Google and enter your page URL and click on 'fetch' to get your page indexed.
6. **Add New Content:** It's a good idea to continually add new content so Google has a reason to keep coming back to your site to crawl new pages.

Improving Site and Page Load Speed

Page speed is an important rank metric so taking measures to improve it and keeping a regular check on it is vital. You can perform routine site speed tests using Pingdoom Tools.

Some of the reasons why your site speed can be slow are:

- Your hosting company
- Too many images or large images
- Use of flash
- Excess plugins
- Excess widgets
- Too many ads
- Using a heavy theme
- External embedded media like videos

Since site speed is one of the Google ranking factors, you need to take measures to improve it if it's slow for your site. Too slow would be categorized as roughly equal to or more than 3 seconds with abandonment rates increased significantly after the 2-second mark. Some ways you can improve your site speed are:

- Reduce redirects to remove additional waiting time

- Use a file compression software to decrease the size of large CSS, JavaScript and HTML files.
- Optimize image load time by adding images in a smaller file to being with instead of having to compress them as that can reduce their quality.
- Use a caching plugin like WP rocket. It will do the heavy lifting for you.
- Remove and reduce the usage of unnecessary widgets and plugins you don't need or no longer use.

Of course, there are more technical ways to fix page speed as well. Once you're done with the above and if your site speed is still above 3 seconds, you can look into other fixes and hire an expert to look into the technical side of things for you.

Off-Page SEO

Off-page SEO, as the name suggests, takes place on external sites instead of on your site and mainly involves link building. It is more time consuming than on-page and also more difficult as everything is not in your control but the results can be phenomenal.

Off-page SEO mainly includes:

1. Link Building
2. Link Earning
3. Social Signals

Link Building Process

Link building is the process of having other sites point to your site. Google sees these links as a signal that your site content is good enough to be linked to. Link building involves building links to your site either by submission, which is at your discretion or by requesting other sites to link to you.

You can check your site's backlinks using backlink checker tools such as Ahrefs and SEMrush. These are both paid tools but very accurate and useful.

Beginners often get confused about where to get their links from and usually resort to the typical methods such as guest posting and directories. But there's so much more to link building. Below I've compiled a massive list of link building ideas:

List of Link Building Ideas

1. **Guest Posting:** Guest posting involves writing articles for other blogs in your

industry with a backlink to your site within the article. This allows those other sites to get good content, and you for you to get a link to your site and incoming traffic from their site. So it's a win-win situation for both. Guest posting is a widely used link building technique. Some say it's dead, spammy and not safe. But if done right, it can add a lot of value. What you need to keep in mind while guest posting is to post on the highest quality sites that are relevant to your industry. The most common approach to guest posting is simply reaching out to influential blog owners in your niche. It's a great idea but getting a guest post to go live on influential blogs is not always easy. These blogs are popular and so receive hundreds of outreach emails a day requesting to guest blog for them. Some of these blogs don't even accept guest posts and clearly state that. However, to get a higher response rate, it is a better idea to reach out to sites that are actually accepting guest posts. You can find these sites quickly using search strings (which have been explained in detail later on). There are also various guest posting communities like Post Joint, Blogger Link Up, etc. that list out sites in need of guest posts, industry wise. Another way to find guest post opportunities is to trace your competitor's backlinks to find out which sites they've written on.

2. **Reverse Guest Posting:** Reverse guest posting involves inviting guest bloggers to blog on your site instead of you on theirs and having them share and link to their article on your site on their site.

3. **Get Students to Blog on University Blogs:** University and college students have access

to the institution's blog portal and can be hired to do an article and drop a link to your site in it.

4. **Unlinked Brand Mentions:** There are many times when site owners talk about your brand but they don't link back. These are called unlinked brand mentions. The fact that they mentioned your business is great but not enough to send over traffic because there is no link. Not many people reading the article will put in the effort to copy your brand name and search it to find your site. A link back is required for traffic purposes and also for backlink purposes. Getting sites with unlinked brand mentions to you to link back is an easy link building method because since those sites are already talking about you, they don't mind linking back since all the work is already done and they already know about you. You can find all of

your unlinked mentions using search strings which have been discussed later on or even at scale in just a few minutes using tools (video tutorials are up on this and other topics in the Digiologist SEO Course).

5. **URL Mentions:** Along with finding brand name mentions, it's also important to find URL mentions, i.e., when sites use your site URL in their article instead of your brand name. Though this is less common, it's still important to go after. The URLs being referred to here are the ones not resulting in hyperlinks due to a missing http:// and so, not resulting in an actual link.

6. **Misspelled Mentions:** If there are more than a few ways to type your company name or even a few possible spelling mistakes, insert them into the tools or search strings to find unlinked mentions with the wrong company name as well. This

should also be done for company name variations and short forms and also former names in case you recently changed your name.

7. **Competitors Brand Mentions:** You can't exactly get a link for your competitors brand mention, but you can track your competitors mentions to see where they're being linked from so you can try getting a link for your site as well.

8. **Track Industry Term Mentions:** Create an alert for popular industry term mentions so you know which sites are talking about specific topics in your industry. Tracking such terms will bring up prospects of sites mentioning them and possible sites and pages you can get a link from by contributing in some way.

9. **Resources:** Resources are pages that are lists of links to companies, products or

services. They're all over the web and exist for practically every industry. Reach out to site owners and request to be included in them.

10. **Competitor Backlink Analysis:** You can use backlink checker tools to get access to the entire backlink profile of your competitors. After getting a list of their backlinks, sort according to quality and relevancy and see which of the sites you can get a link from as well.

11. **Ranking Pages Backlink Analysis:** From an SEO perspective, all sites ranking above you in the search engines for your preferred keywords are competitors. Most businesses think of their competitors mostly in the offline sense. But from an SEO perspective, any site that ranks above you for a preferred keyword is your competitor. Take the exact pages that rank above you and get

a list of the backlinks pointing to them (not to the entire domain, but pointing to the actual pages only) and see which ones you can get a link from for yourself.

12. **Broken Link Building:** There are many sites out there linking out to broken pages that are either to sites that were shut down or pages that just don't exist anymore. You can find these pages at scale for sites in your industry using broken link checker tools and inform the webmasters and request your link to be added instead of it.

13. **Blog Badge:** Create a blog badge and inform your readers. Your most loyal readers will share it on their sites and link back to you.

14. **Get Local Library Links:** Libraries usually have a link page on their site to act as a resource for the general public as a compilation of professionals from different industries. Check out your local library's

website and see if you can get listed on it as well.

15. **Question and Answer Site Commenting:** These links aren't the highest quality for backlink purposes but they can be huge for increasing incoming traffic. Q and A sites like Quora for example get a large number of visitors each month so build a presence there. Find questions related to your industry that have been asked and answer them. When you answer a question, you end up being perceived as the expert and get a backlink to your site. If you provide value to others through helpful answers, they'll make their way to your site.

16. **Get Your Own Wikipedia Page:** If you've built enough authority, get yourself a Wikipedia page. Just have someone else write it for you so it's natural and is unbiased.

17. **Interlinking:** Interlinking is not off-site but can still add a lot of value and help in ranking. It involves crosslinking your sites internal pages to each other. Since the links are coming from your site, you have the authority to choose their location and anchor text so take advantage of that. You can link from your highest ranking and most visited pages to pages you want to boost, to your ranking pages to help increase their ranking further or to important landing pages.

18. **Link Roundups:** These are compilations of great links on a certain topic you can put together on your blog. These can be lists of great articles that recently came up in your industry or links to niche influencers sites. After you're done publishing your roundup, contact the people linked to in it. They will appreciate the mention and most will either

link back to your roundup article or at least socially share it.

19. **Forum Link Building:** Forums are online discussion threads created for a specific industries where people post threads to ask questions, ask for opinions or to simply just post their opinion to discuss a particular topic. You can become a member of some of the forums in your industry and join in on the conversations taking place.

20. **Blog Commenting:** This is something a lot of people do naturally. We all read many blog posts a day to do our share of industry reading. Why not leave a comment after reading while you're on the page? Many commenting systems such as Disqus allow links in the user profiles, so you end up automatically getting a backlink in each comment.

21. **Getting Trackbacks:** When you link to other bloggers from your blog articles and source them as relevant blog posts or references, you can fill their link in the trackback section. This then leaves a trackback (also called pingback) on the other bloggers article in the comments section as a link and short summary to your article. These may not always appear instantly though as some bloggers like to manually approve them. But either way, they're great for not only gaining backlinks but also relationship building.

22. **Job Postings:** Many times business owners rely on filling positions through referrals and don't post job openings online. It's a good idea to take advantage of the opening and post it on high traffic job sites so you can get a backlink as well.

23. **Add A Snippet Feature to Your Content:** Uploading your content online will attract people copying your content no matter what. People will right click and save and re-publish elsewhere. A trick to try to get a link while they do that is adding snippets to your content. That way, along with picking up your content, the person also copies a link back (and also a short summary) to your site along with it.

24. **Blogrolls:** Blogrolls are lists of blog owners recommended blogs. While it may be tough to get on someone's blogroll without knowing them at first, it's a good idea to build a relationship and introduce them to your blog so they see the value in adding it to their roll.

25. **Expired Domain Link Building:** Sites expire and shut down all the time. You can take advantage of that and either purchase

those domains and redirect them to your site or simply check their backlinks and request the sites linking to them to link to you instead. This only works and is worth doing if the expired sites are in the same industry as you and have SEO value. It can work with sites in adjacent industries as well. These links are also easy to get because the site owners are informed they're linking to expired domains so they're interested in either removing the link or replacing it with a another relevant link which can be with your link in exchange for the help.

26. **Non-existent Service Pages:** Find pages or sites that used to offer a service but no longer do and request to have their backlinks pointed to your site instead. Businesses get shut down or have some of their products/services closed down all the

time. If you find out about something halted in your industry and the particular page or site that used to represent it has a good number of backlinks, inform the site owners they're linking to a removed product/service and have them replace the link to your existing product instead.

27. **Expired Blogspot Blogs with Good Backlinks:** Blogspot is a blogging platform providing free hosting. It uses a .blogspot domain that looks something like: www.example.blogspot.com. The great thing about Blogspot is when a user shuts down their blog, their Blogspot address is available for anyone to register. And it's free. You can take advantage of that by registering closed down Blogpost addresses that had some good backlinks. And since Blogspot is a Google product, its links have

good value and can help create a good web 2.0 strategy.

28. **Moved Sites:** Some businesses move to other site addresses, leaving their old domain behind. Register any such sites from your industry that have a good backlink profile and use them to your advantage. You can either use those domains for building a site and linking to yourself from it, or simply redirecting it to a relevant page on your site.

29. **Link Poaching:** Link poaching involves having your competitors backlinks replaced to links pointing to your site instead. If you can provide sites that are linking to your competitors sites with better content to link to on your site instead and replace the links, just think of it as adding more value to those sites for their readers.

30. **Link Re-purposing:** This isn't a technique to build new fresh links, but rather repurpose old ones. You may have most of your links pointing to your homepage or even an old landing page that might not even exist anymore. You can reach out to the site owners linking to you and have them link to a different page instead that's a more important internal page. It's a good idea to have your links pointing to your homepage as well as deeper internal pages. But if too many of them point to your homepage, go for some diversity and request some of them to be changed.

31. **Link Reclamation:** Some of the links you previously built or earned may go missing with time. This could be due to pages removed from the sites of previous linkers or they could go lost during their site redesign processes. You can always reach

out to them and ask for a link inclusion again in some way. You don't have to manually keep a check on this. Upload all links built and earned into Raven Tools and it will automatically notify you each time a link is removed.

32. **Phone-Based Link Building:** Not exactly a link building method but this idea works extremely well. When you request for a link through a phone call rather than an email, it's a lot easier make the relationship and get the link as you can be more personable and communicate better over phone. It's not possible to pick up the phone for each link you're trying to build so do this for the top sites you're trying to get a link from.

33. **Display Ads:** Display ads through banners on other sites get you an immediate link. While this may be a short-term image link, it's still worth experimenting with. This can

allow you get a link on some of the best blogs in your industry and for a much lower price than if you directly asked them for a sponsored link quote. This is also really good for increasing traffic and leads.

34. **Reclaim External Profile Link Pages:** People will link to you if they like your product without you even requesting a link. But at times, such naturally earned links can end up pointing to your social profiles instead of your website and while getting a link to your social media is great, it's a good idea to reclaim links to your social profiles to point to your website instead.

35. **Reclaim Links Pointing to 404 Pages:** If you've been making some site changes recently and deleted or moved some pages, you may now have a few 404 not found pages. Check to see if there are any backlinks pointing to them and have them

changed to point to the more updated pages on your site instead.

36. **Content Gaps:** Filling content gaps involves improving the content on topics in your industry on other sites. There's plenty of content out there that's incomplete or outdated and could use some additions to improve it. You being an industry expert can reach out to those sites with additional information and be quoted as a source and score yourself a link.

37. **Content Link Replacements:** This is similar to link poaching, except that it doesn't involve stealing your competitors links but just links to other content. Find content in your industry that ranks well and you have a substitute for on your blog, get a list of its backlinks, reach out to the sites linking to that content and let them know you have a similar article that is a better and a more

updated version that they can link to it instead.

38. **Create Great Content and Ask for Links:** One of the simplest ways of link building is to just create link worthy content that earns links naturally because people want to link to it. Create assets that will attract links. This could be in the form of eBooks, white papers, infographics, guides or just well written blog articles. It doesn't have to be super fancy and lengthy. Just provide value and make it better than your competitors so people see why they should link to you.

39. **Blog Post Translation:** If your blog is in English, have some of your blog posts shared on other sites in other countries in other languages after translation. This can be like a guest article, except you're not writing new content but just repurposing old content and making it new through

translation. You can also cross-link one another using hreflang tags. This is great for businesses that have their product/service available worldwide so they can target audiences in other countries.

40. **Infographics:** Have a few infographics designed each year that are high quality and unique so they're shareable and stand out from all the other infographics out there so people want to share them. After having them designed reach out to site owners and allow them to use the graphics on their site with a link back. You can also do some infographic submission on infographic sites.

41. **Memes:** Memes may not be suitable for all businesses but if your business isn't too formal, give memes a try instead in addition to other graphics like infographics and

reach out to site owners and allow them to use them provided they give you a backlink.

42. **Info-animations:** Info-animations are short animated videos and are made with the same goal infographics are made with: to explain complex topics in an easier way. These are something that not everyone is doing so other sites will be interested in embedding them on their site.

43. **Periodic 'Best of' List:** Create an ongoing 'best of' list either each week or month where you link to the best articles or overall blogs from your industry by compiling them into a list. This is like a roundup and similar to article roundups that are one question interview style, except that with this strategy you're creating a list style compilation of your favorite links. After creating and publishing it, reach out to the people you mentioned in it and let them

know you gave them a shoutout on your site. This will allow you to build a relationship with them and at times they will link back to the list they've been mentioned in or return the favour through a backlink some other way.

44. **Blog Carnival:** Blog carnivals are like link submission parties, except that the link needs to be to an article. Blog carnivals, which are sometimes also called blog parties, have a theme or topic announced beforehand and ask for bloggers to submit articles links talking about that topic. If you participate and submit a link to your article on that topic, you get an immediate link.

45. **Blog Incubation:** Blog incubation involves starting your own blogs to get links from. This refers to blogs separate from your main site. These are like mini blogs you make just to cross-link and are great

because you get to grow your audience and choose your link anchor text.

46. **Check Copyscape for Copied Content:** Everything you put out on the web has a chance of being copied. Keep a check on which of your content gets copied and posted on other sites. If you're sensitive about it you can just ask those site owners to remove the content. But if you're more concerned with getting a link, reach out to the sites and ask for your site to be linked to and quoted as the source of that content.

47. **Content Curation:** Content curation involves finding the best content on the web, compiling it and sharing it with your network. There are various sites you can use for this. Create an account on them and post curated content regularly to build a following. Once you've created a following,

you then have access to a network of people interested in your industry that you can post your content to whenever you need to.

48. **Web 2.0 Sites:** This involves creating a presence on web 2.0 sites like Tumblr, Blogger, Wordpress etc. Web 2.0 sites are like free blogging platforms. You can put relevant content on them by outsourcing articles or through article spinning. Once you've built up authority and a readership on your web 2.0 properties, you can start adding links in them pointing to your main site. These links will be relevant and all in your control so you get to choose their location and anchor text.

49. **Contact People Using Your Images:** Similar to using Copyscape to check people using your content, use image source checker tools like TinEye to find people who've used

your images without your permission. You can reach out to them to have them add a backlink to your site and quote you as the source for the image.

50. **Image Embed Codes:** Similar to using snippets for content, add image embed code options for every image. This will give people the option of using the images on their site using the embed code instead of saving and uploading them. This also straight away gives them permission and encourages them to use the images and you automatically get a backlink from the embed codes.

51. **Offer Images to be Used With Credit:** In addition to providing image embed codes and getting credit from those using your images without permission, it's also a good idea to simply offer your images for use. When you offer them, more people will

know they're available for use and they're more likely to end up being used, resulting in more links obtained.

52. **PR Commenting:** Make an account on PR commenting sites like HARO (Help a Reporter Out) and Response Source. These sites have a lot of journalists sign up that are looking for opinions from specialists in different fields. You get all of the questions/topics that replies are required for from journalists and you can answer the ones related to your industry. If the journalist finds your answer useful, they use it in their article and quote you and link back to your site. At times you can get links from very reputable sites such as Huffington Post, Forbes etc. that is otherwise quite difficult.

53. **Get Interviewed:** You can reach out to sites in your city and offer to be interviewed or

find interview opportunities through PR sites. You can also follow the interview path of your competitors to see which sites they've been interviewed on and try to score an one for yourself there as well.

54. **Give Product/Service for Review:** Give your product or offer your service to influential bloggers to try out and review on their site.

55. **Give Products/Service Away in a Giveaway:** Give away your product or service in a giveaway or contest on your site. You can set sharing your site socially or writing a blog post about an industry topic with a link to your site at the bottom as the rules for entry. This way, all the participants will link back to your site in order to get an entry to the contest so you end up getting multiple links.

56. **Contest/Giveaway on Other Bloggers Sites:** In addition to giving away your

product/service on your site, offer to give it as a prize for other bloggers giveaways with a rule for entry being either sharing your site socially or linking back to your site through a blog post. This way, all the participants will link back to your site in order to get an entry to the contest and so you end up getting multiple links.

57. **Ask People You Know for a Link:** Think about all the contacts you've built through that have their own businesses you can get a link from.

58. **Associations/Organizations:** Get a link from associations or organizations in your industry you're a part of. They usually have a members page.

59. **Awards:** Get a link from sites of committees or organizations your business got awards from in the past.

60. **Offer a Scholarship:** Offer a scholarship to students from different universities having writing an essay as the criteria for entry. The students will post their essay on their blog (and create blogs on free blogging platforms in case they don't have one) and link to your site as the source of the scholarship as the rule for entry.
61. **Offer Student Discounts:** Offering student discounts is a great way to get links from university and college sites, backlinks from which are considered high in value.
62. **Sponsor Events:** Build relationships by sponsoring local events. The event sponsors are shown on the event site and usually linked to.
63. **Volunteering:** Volunteer to help out local charities, NGOs, organizations. This helps build relationships and it's easier getting links with those relationships. Most such

organizations have a members page on their site which they use to link to participating companies.

64. **Donations:** Through donations you build relationships as philanthropy work is always appreciated. Organizations that accept donations usually have a donators list on their site where you can have yourself added and linked to after giving the donation.

65. **Testimonials:** Reach out to the sites of products/services you regularly use for your business and offer to provide a testimonial for their site. They'll not only use it and give you a link back from it to your site, but also appreciate it and easily accept it.

66. **Submissions:** The methods below all refer to getting the link by manually submitting your assets to gain a link on directories or submission sites.

- Industry directories
- Article submission
- Image submission
- Infographic submission
- Slides submission
- Social bookmarking
- Video submission
- Press release submission
- Profile links

Building High Quality Links

While building links using the tactics above, here's what to aim for to ensure your links are high quality:

1. They're on sites that are relevant and in your niche
2. Are do-follow
3. Use relevant and keyword rich anchor text

4. From authority sites with good traffic and engagement
5. High on-page social shares
6. Editorial links are always the best

The relevancy factor is key here as you shouldn't just be concerned with only building the link and sending a signal to Google but also look into the possible traffic that'll come in through the link, and you want it to be relevant. Having the link set to do-follow will ensure Google sees it so make sure you try to convert no-follow links to do-follow because they won't pass any link juice.

You can get a bit of an idea of the authority of the site by checking their DA, i.e., domain authority. I don't entirely rely on DA when evaluating a site because it can be artificially inflated, so a better idea is to look into their social profiles and engagement by checking how many comments they get on their posts etc.

Editorial vs. Passive Links

Editorial links are higher quality than passive links. Editorial links are links within content and are usually built by conducting outreach. Passive links are lower quality links you can manually build such as forum and directory links. The easier it is to get a link, the lower quality it usually is.

Importance of Link Anchor Text

Anchor text is the visible, clickable text on a link. It's the word or group of words that you click on to open a link. The anchor text used for the links you build are important and powerful so having your targeted keywords as the anchor text of your links helps you rank for them. Google takes the anchor text to be the description of the link, and thus, the description of the content of the page, thereby increasing your chances of ranking for such terms.

Although anchor text is powerful, it can also have a negative effect if exact anchor texts are repeatedly used for many links as that's seen as being spammy. To avoid overuse of specific keywords as anchor text, use different keywords or variations of your main keyword. Of course when you're building links through outreach, choosing the anchor text is at the discretion of the person giving you the link, so your choice of anchor text is not always guaranteed and the most you can do is simply request it. Often times the site owner ends up giving you generic anchor text such as 'site', 'here' etc. or simply a URL link, so it's not of any danger.

Types of Anchor Text

Below are some of the different anchor texts you can have:

1. **Branded:** This would be using your business or product name as the anchor text. Most links with non-generic anchor text end up taking this format.
2. **Exact Match Targeted Keyword:** This would be an exact match of the main keywords you're trying to rank for. Overuse of the exact match of your targeted keywords as anchor text is seen as spammy and can lead to penalties. It's recommended you stick to 10% of your anchor texts as an exact match only to be on safe side.
3. **Secondary Keywords:** These are all keywords other than your main keywords, and since there's a much larger amount of

secondary keywords, you can use each of these as exact matches more than once, and you'll never run out of anchor text ideas.

4. **Partial Match:** Using partial match anchors is a great way to target your main keywords without getting penalized as it involves combining your main keywords with other text so it doesn't result in an exact match. For example, if your main targeted keyword is 'personal injury lawyer', you can turn it into partial match anchor ideas such as personal injury lawyer Toronto, personal injury lawyer consultation, personal injury lawyer benefits, personal injury lawyer case studies, etc. That way you still get to target your main keywords, but with the addition of extra text on to it, you don't face the risk of penalization as it leads to targeting

various keywords instead of the overuse of one.

5. **URL:** It's a good idea to mix in simple URL links from time to time wherein the URL itself acts as the anchor text. This helps gain some diversity in your anchor text portfolio so it appears natural and not too constructed.

6. **Generic:** You'll end up getting generic anchor text links either from other sites, from links naturally earned or when you manually build them on directories and profiles. Some examples of generic anchor text are site, here, website, click here, etc. The anchor text isn't given much thought in such cases and is chosen just to link to another site. While generic anchors don't help in specific keyword targeting, they still end up resulting in a link which is useful and

help in anchor text diversity, leading it to appear natural and not forced.

Aim to have a good mix of branded links, naked links, and anchor text links. This makes your anchor text portfolio appear natural. There's no need to calculate anchor text usage percentages manually as you can easily check them out using a backlink checker tool like SEMrush.

It's also good to have your links point to a variety of different pages on your site. It's natural to have the majority of your backlinks point to your home page because most times the home page is the most relevant page to represent the brand overall and most naturally earned links point to the homepage. But try gaining links to deeper internal pages as well for diversity and where you're trying to link pages other than the homepage.

No-follow vs. Do-follow Links

A link can either be do-follow or no-follow. A do-follow link passes link value, and a no-follow link doesn't as it's not seen or considered by search engines. In short, a no-follow link has no value in terms of SEO. But that doesn't mean they're completely useless as they bring in traffic. It's also a good idea to have a diverse link portfolio containing a mixture of do-follow and no-follow links, as it appears more natural. The decision of whether a link is to be do-follow or no-follow is made by the site owner who creates the link, so it's not always at your discretion. You can easily check whether a link is do-follow or no-follow using the Mozbar browser add-on. It highlights all do-follow and no-follow links on any page in different colors so you can spot no-follow ones easily.

Changing a Link from Do-follow to No-follow and Vice Versa:

Most links are automatically set to do-follow and their script looks like:
<ahref="https://www.site.com"rel="dofollow">Anchor Text</a>

To change it to no-follow, simply locate the script in Wordpress and change to:

<ahref=https://www.site.com"rel="nofollow">Anchor Text</a>

The Process of Sending Outreach Emails

Tips: While link building, in many cases to get a backlink you'll have to contact site owners and request it. Some of these site owners get hundreds of emails a month with requests for being added to a resource page on their site, to submit a guest post, etc. Your email has to stand out so it's not rejected. Your subject line is the first thing the webmaster sees so make it attractive enough so they open your email. A small part of the beginning of your email is also visible to them before they even open your email so make that part click-worthy too.

Try sending emails from a personal name rather than using the company name, as people are more likely to open it then. It's important to keep your message short and to explain the value that they're getting as well. I've provided some examples of my tried and tested emails later on that you can use.

Finding Contact Information: While searching for the contact information of prospects you want a link from, you'll notice that the email given on the website about page is usually a generic email such as info@example.com or contact@example.com and mostly not for a specific person. You can contact that email and usually receive a response, but there are higher chances of getting a link if you reach the right person so try looking around on their site for the contact info of an exact person instead. If you know the name of the person you want to contact, you can usually get their email through a Google search.

Open Rates: To see if the emails you're sending out are being opened, you can use tools such as Yesware or the Yet Another Mail Merge add on for Google Sheets before sending out your emails.

Scaling the Outreach Process

Mass Outreach: If there's a fixed email template you want to stick to and send to a list of people while only customizing a few fields such as their name and site mention, you can save a significant amount of time and effort by sending your emails in bulk through.

Create the template you want to email and send it in bulk to everyone on your list using a mail merge tool such as Yet Another Mail Merge for Google Sheets. It will even update the sheet automatically to show who opened the email and at what times.

You can also use email finder tools to scale the process and make it faster. One that I use and recommend is called Email Hunter.

Outreach Tips

Many of the above link building ideas consist of conducting outreach. And the best method for doing so is through email. It's fast and cheap, and you can quickly reach a wide audience. I've sent emails on behalf of hundreds of clients in the past to gain links through a variety of methods such as unlinked brand mentions, resource pages, guest posts, broken links, media placements, etc. and it has worked very well. As long as you're reaching out to relevant sites, a large number of sites and using a good email template, you'll find success. On average, most people gain around five links for every hundred emails they send, so a 5% success rate. I've monitored success rates for my clients in the past and depending on the relevancy of the sites prospected and emails of contacts found, I've been able to achieve 12-15% as well.

The tips to follow are the same for every email no matter what the link strategy you're applying. Your email template should have:

1. **Good Subject Line:** In addition to measuring the success rate, you should also measure your open rates, i.e., total emails opened

compared to total sent. The most significant factor leading to high open rates is a good subject line. Make sure your subject line is short, to the point, interesting and click-worthy and doesn't seem spammy. Also, ensure that whatever subject line you choose is completely visible when you send it and not cut off. You can send yourself a test email using that subject line to see if it's entirely visible and how it looks.

2. **Interesting Initial Email Content:** In some email hosts, you can see the first 1-2 sentences of the email before you even open it as they're shown next to the subject line, so make them interesting to increase open rates.

3. **Short and to the Point:** In most cases, shorter is better. People don't have time to read long emails, and they especially won't

devote that time to you if it's your first interaction with them.

4. **Value They're Receiving:** A common mistake is to ask ask ask. Make the email about the value the site owner will be getting from providing the link as well.

5. **Address the Correct Name:** A mistake many people make is either not addressing the person they're emailing by their name, misspelling their name, addressing them only by their last name or the incorrect person. All of this makes the email appear unprofessional, spammy and as if it was sent using a mass email sending software and leads to close rates.

Email Templates

Below are a few examples of email templates for a few different link strategies. Build off of them for other strategies and modify and test as you go along.

Guest Post Outreach:

Subject Line: *Have Some Article Ideas for Your Blog*

Hi Name,

My name is _____ and I'm the Founder at _____ , a _____ (add a brief info to your site).

I'm contacting to you as I'd love to write a guest post for you and be featured on your blog. I am looking to contribute to high-quality blogs and being featured on your end would be an honor.

Here are some Ideas I had for articles:

- *Article idea 1*
- *Article idea 2*
- *Article idea 3*

Please let me know which topic interests you the most. If there's a different topic you need, I can write that for you as well.

Here are some links to content I've previously written:

- *Link 1*
- *Link 2*
- *Link 3*

Let me know which article you'd like me to send over. Looking forward to working with you!

Name

Unlinked Brand Mentions

Subject Line: *Thanks for mentioning _____ (company name) in your article, but you forgot something*

Hi Name,

I was browsing your website when I noticed that you'd mentioned us here: Link

It's great to see us featured on a great site like yours! It would be even more awesome if a link back to our site could be added to the article.

Here is the page you can link back to: www.yoursite.com

Please let me know if you need any more information.

Thanks,

Name

Scholarship Campaign:

Subject Line: *We'd like to provide your students with a $____ (amount) Scholarship*

Hi *Name*,

We are writing to inform you that we at _____are providing a $_____ scholarship opportunity to any of your previously graduated, current or future students.

We are _____ (brief intro to your company and why you'd like to provide the scholarship).

Here is the link to our scholarship details and rules for participation: Link

It would be great if our scholarship details could be added to your page here: Link

That would allow us to give a greater amount of students the chance to participate!

Please let us know if you have any questions. We look forward to reading submissions from your students.

Thanks,

Name

Using Search Strings for Link Prospecting

Search strings are a combination of keywords, characters, and modifiers that make conducting more detailed Google searches a lot easier. They make searching for link opportunities easier and faster. When you're searching for something specific and only want particular results, using search strings can help significantly.

Here are some modifiers you can add to your keywords to create search strings to conduct detailed searches:

1. " "

The quotation marks modifier yields exact results based on whatever is inserted in the quotations. Whether you insert an entire search phrase in the quotes or a just a part of it, whatever it encloses is what the search engine is told to search for as an exact match of the word(s).

2. **AND**

The AND modifier can be used to combine two key phrases to ensure both of them are part of the search results instead of one or either or.

3. –

The subtract modifier excludes any word(s) you don't want to be part of the search results.

4. **OR**

Used to get search results for either of multiple terms, i.e., either of two or more keyphrases but not necessarily all of them.

5. **Inurl:**

Looks for the presence of the keywords you're searching in the URLs of different sites rather than the content.

6. **Intitle:**

Looks for pages with the key phrase in the page title. Search:

Search String Examples

Below are some examples of search strings using modifiers to find link building opportunities:

Example: Suppose you're a personal trainer and in the health industry and you'd like to guest post on other sites for building links to your site.

A search string you can use to find guest posting opportunities in the health industry is:

health "guest post" OR "guest author" OR "guest blogger" OR "guest article" OR "submit" OR "write for us"

You can then swap the keyword 'health' for other keywords such as:

fitness "guest post" OR "guest author" OR "guest blogger" OR "guest article" OR "submit" OR "write for us"

weight loss "guest post" OR "guest author" OR "guest blogger" OR "guest article" OR "submit" OR "write for us"

The above is an example of just one of the search strings you can create to find guest post opportunities faster and easier. You can create them for various finding prospective sites for other link building tactics as well such as unlinked brand mentions, resource pages, etc.

Check Your Link Profile for Spammy Backlinks

Don't just wait to be hit with a penalty or to receive a manual notification. Check your backlink profile from time to time to keep a check on spammy backlinks you've acquired naturally. Sort through them and do a disavow to prevent any damage.

Link Earning Strategies

The strategies in the earlier list were link building strategies. But what every marketer should aim for is link earning. Link earning is the automatic acquisition of backlinks without manually building them, i.e., all links you received when people naturally linked to your content without you asking them to. This happens when your content is good and provides value and sites want to link to you.

Here are some ideas for different kinds of content you can generate for your site to serve as link bait that people find value from and link to naturally over time:

1. Overall high-quality content through blog articles
2. Glossary
3. Resource Pages
4. Interviews with Influencers
5. eBooks
6. Whitepapers
7. Research Papers
8. Market Studies
9. Infographics

10. Videos
11. Tools
12. Widgets
13. Softwares
14. Free downloadable assets
15. Podcasts
16. Recorded webinars
17. Powerpoint Slides
18. Quizzes
19. FAQs page

Social Media and SEO

Social signals are significant for SEO and important ranking factors. A higher number of shares of your pages across social platforms increases their chances of ranking. You can take matters into your own hands by building a social presence online by opening up profiles on popular social platforms and by always sharing your newly published new posts across them. Some popular social platforms you can get started on are:

- Facebook
- Twitter
- Pinterest
- Google+

Many people ignore Google+, but it being a Google product is huge for SEO.

Besides you sharing your content across your social platforms, it's a good idea to have your customers do some of the work as well by having them share your content. An easy way to get that started is to have social share icons on all your pages so users can easily share it.

SEO and social media go hand in hand. Likes, shares, tweets, re-tweets, etc. across social platforms provide backlinks as well as important 'signals' that result in higher ranks.

Local SEO

Local SEO involves applying SEO techniques to rank in local search results that provide relevant results to users based on their location and rank for location-specific keywords. For example, if a user located in New York searches for the term 'ice cream shops' and gets ice cream shops located in the UK as results, it wouldn't be useful at all right? Local SEO makes sure users get results relevant to their location.

Local SEO practices are important for businesses that have a fixed physical location or multiple locations. It allows you to be visible to local customers in local search results and appear in map results as well which is important because it shows your location and contact information and is visible to people looking for your business while they're out and about. Local SEO is powerful because it not only allows you to rank in the organic listing results, but also the knowledge graph and map pack as well.

Local SEO involves making efforts in the following areas

1. Google My Business page
2. Citation building
3. Reviews on local platform profiles
4. Local content and on-site on-page optimization with geo-targeted keywords
5. Location pages
6. Links from local sites

Google My Business Page

You need to set up your Google My Business page to avail the benefits of local SEO. You can get started at www.google.com/business . Setting up your GMB page is quite easy. Just follow the steps on adding all of your information such as business name, category, address, phone number, operating hours, business photos, your website link, business description. In case your business has multiple locations, you can add their info in bulk by importing a file. The information in your GMB profile is important as it will show up in the map pack and Knowledge Graph so ensure critical info like your address, phone number, website link and hours of operation are always correct and up to date.

In addition to Google My Business, you should set up a Bing Places profile for each of your locations as well. Bing accounts for 20% of all online searches! While that may not be as much as Google, it is still a significant chunk and something you shouldn't overlook. Bing Places is also not as widely used as Google My Business, which means there is less competition and a greater chance for you to stand out. You can create a Bing Places account at www.bingplaces.com .

Creating a Google My Business page will allow you to:

1. Show up in the Knowledge Graph:

2. Show up in the Map Pack a.k.a Local Pack:

Without a GMB page, you stand no chance of ranking in the local pack and in knowledge graph format so, you end up missing on a chunk of the ranking opportunities., thus, it's very important that you create one for each of your locations.

Citation Building

Citations are an important part of local SEO and require citation building, similar to link building. A citation is an online reference to your business NAP on external sites. NAP is an acronym for the name, address and phone number and that's exactly what a citation is: your business name, address and phone number combination. Citation building is similar to link building except that citations don't link to your site as they're not clickable as they're just the NAP in text format. Regardless, they're seen by Google and taken into consideration for local results.

The way it's similar to link building is that it involves the process of building as many citations on external sites as possible. You can do this by building profiles on local directories and adding your citations there.

Citation Format

Here is a commonly used format for citations:

Company Name,
Company Address,
City,
State/Province,
Postal Code/Zip Code
Phone Number

The above format can be changed around as well, as long as they make sense and are in the right order. For example, you can have the city and state/province in one line together as well or have the city, state/province as well as zip/postal code all on one line. As long as it is a NAP combination in the right order and is unchanged for all your citations, it's fine.

Here's an example of how an actual citation would look like:

ABC Solutions,
72 Highland Ridge,
Midvale,
Utah,
84073
(801)3467-9652

Putting your NAP together is quite easy, but complications arise when there's no consistency in your citations. The way you initially decide to format your NAP is exactly how each citation needs to be built to avoid inconsistencies. If you decide to change your address, company name or phone number in the future, it's important to update your past citations as well to avoid NAP inconsistencies. Citation inconsistency can cause ranking issues so locate and remove inconsistent NAPs. Storing the login info while creating citations is important so you can easily update your NAPs if any part of your NAP is changed later on.

You can find citation opportunities through manual searches as well as by using tools such as Whitespark. You can also track your local rankings for different location based keywords using tools like Georanker and Brightlocal.

You can also a competitor citation analysis to track where your competitors are getting their citations from, just like you can check their backlinks in the case of link building. Track your competitor's citation sources using the above mentioned tools. To get a bit of an idea where your competitor's citations are coming from, you can also do a manual search without any tools. To do that, just Google the competitor's name and zip/postal code together, and you'll get results of all of the pages with their citations.

Reviews on Local Profiles

Getting favorable reviews and a good overall star rating is important for local SEO as a ranking factor for the map pack and knowledge graph results. Good reviews and ratings on Google from your customers will not only help you rank, but also influence people to click through to your site and make purchases.

So after each transaction is over, send your customers an email to request them to leave a review and include a short list of the steps on leaving a review to avoid any confusion and to make the process faster.

Below is an email template I've used in the past successfully:

Subject line: *Please review _____ (company name). We'd love your feedback!*

Hello Name,

We'd appreciate it if you could take out some time to review _____ (company name) on Google. We really value your feedback!

Leaving a review on Google is very easy and just requires 3 simple steps:

Step 1: Be signed into your Gmail account. If you don't have a Gmail, here are the steps on creating one. (link to the Gmail support page)
Step 2: Click the following link to open the review box: link

Step 3: Click 'post' and you're done!

Your review is important and will help others as well. Thank you once again!

Name

On-Site Optimization for Local

On-site optimization for local SEO includes:

1. Creation of pages for your location(s) served
2. Creating pages targeting local keywords with location modifiers
3. Adding your NAP (i.e., Name, Address, Phone Number) to your site footer

Add your NAP to every page of your site in the footer. If you're unsure of how to format your NAP, see the citation building section below.

Keyword Research for Local SEO

The process of finding location based keywords is the same as while finding general non-location modifier keywords. The use of tools will help you out significantly. In most keyword research tools, you have the option of inputting the location you want the keywords found for. Once you input your seed keywords, it comes back with many keywords with location modifiers attached.

Target geo-targeted keywords on your site with specific content for that purpose. These will show up while doing keyword research based on what people are already searching. Add them to your page titles, URL, page content, etc. like you usually do on-page SEO.

Also, make a page on your site for each location in case of multi-location businesses and have your URL structures reflect that so these pages can rank for location-specific searches. E.g., if your business has locations in New York, Los Angeles and Chicago, set your pages to:

www.example.com/locations/new-york
www.example.com/locations/los-angeles
www.example.com/locations/chicago

Building Local Links

Build as many links and citations on local sites as possible. These are sites in your city like city-specific blogs, news sites, and directories. Find these sites manually using search strings by adding local modifiers and citation finder tools like White Spark.

How Google Decides What to Rank

Now that we've gone into on-page, off-page and local in detail, let's look at some of the Google ranking factors. Google works in giving the user a list of the most accurate results from its database for the search query inputted. Let's demonstrate the power of search engines with the help of an example. If you open Google and type in the term 'car dealer'. The .com version of Google brings back 170 million results in less than a second! Yet, Google was still able to rank all 170 million of those sites and even chose one of them to rank #1. How did it decide all that?

Google has a long list of ranking factors it considers, some of which are:

- Keyword usage on-page
- Title tag
- Backlinks
- Content length
- Time spent on page
- Direct site visits
- Domain age and authority
- Social shares
- Site speed
- Click through rate in SERPs
- Bounce rate

The above are just some of the factors. There are over 100 of them, a complete list of which can be found online.

Assessing Results

There are many different factors you can look into while assessing SEO success, some of which are:

- Organic traffic
- Bounce rate
- Time spent on site
- Average pages viewed per session
- Click through rate
- Rankings
- Backlinks acquired

The three main tools you need to keep a check the results of your work are:

1. Google Analytics
2. Google Search Console
3. A rank tracker and backlink checker tool like SEMrush

The first two are free, so there's no reason you shouldn't have an account on them. Tools can become a bit information heavy so below are some metrics you can look at in them and what they mean:

Google Analytics

Google Analytics is a powerful tool that gives you a massive amount of data for your site such as the number of visitors, average visit duration, the locations visits are coming from, sources and much more.

Below is a screenshot of a GA dashboard and some of the common terms it uses explained:

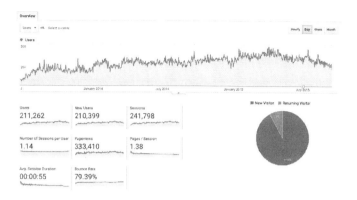

Sessions: Group of user interactions with your site that take place within time-based expiration based on either 30 minutes of inactivity or midnight, whichever takes place earlier.

Pageviews: The total number of pages viewed on your site.

Users: Visitors to your website, which are further classified by GA as new vs. returning.

Average Sessions Per User: Average sessions that took place based on users that visited.

Pages/Session: The average of the pages viewed for the total sessions that took place.

Average Session Duration: The average time the sessions lasted.

Bounce Rate: The percentage of one-page visits.

Active Users: The number of users that visited your site either within the past 30 days or the last 30 days of the data chosen.

Lifetime Value: Shows how useful visitors are to your business based on lifetime performance which is calculated keeping in mind different metrics like goal completions per user, revenue per user, etc.

Cohort Analysis: Involves the segmentation of users based on a date like date of acquisition, date of first transaction completion, etc.

Affinity Categories: Audiences that are actively searching and comparing your product/service.

In-Market Segments: Analyzes a user's overall interests and passions to get a better understanding of their identity.

Engagement: Number of engaged visits to the site based on bounce rate, pages/visit, and average visit duration.

Frequency vs. Recency: Frequency measures the number of visits per each user to your site and recency measures the number of days that have passed on since their last visit.

Acquisition Channels: The different sources your site visitors were acquired form such as direct, organic, referral, social, pay per click, etc.

Behavior Flow: Shows the path your users use to travel your site's pages from the first page they land on to the one they exit from.

ORGANIC SEARCH POSITIONS 1 - 100 (606)

Keyword	Pos.	Volume	KD	CPC (USD)
fossil watch	31	27,100	80.73	0.56
silver jewelry	6 (9)	320	63.72	1.18
costume jewelry toronto	3 (5)	170	51.24	1.08
wedding hair pieces	9 (45)	480	59.33	0.56
bittersweet boutique	2 (3)	90	60.11	0.00

The above screenshot is from SEMrush, which is a good one that gives you a wide variety of data that GA doesn't provide like organic keywords ranking and their positions and URLs.

Doing SEO without a good SEO tool will make it difficult to check on ranks and do in-depth keyword research. So along with the free but very powerful Google Analytics and Search Console, invest in one paid SEO tool of choice to track ranking positions and find keywords.

Dealing With Penalties and Algorithmic Changes

Search engines change their algorithms, i.e., ranking factors from time to time to improve their results and prevent irrelevant lower quality websites from ranking.

When a new algorithm change takes place, your website could get hit and lose its rankings if you were partaking spammy black hat SEO activities. It's strongly recommended you never participate in black hat tactics as Google will always find out and you will get penalized.

White Hat vs. Black Hat SEO:

White hat SEO contains all of the SEO practices that comply with search engine regulations. These practices are not spammy and aim to prove value to users. Blackhat, on the other hand, involves practices that are not in compliance with search engine regulations and involve manipulation to rank.

An example of doing the same work through white hat and black hat methods can be explained with the case of link building. An example of a white hat approach to building links would be through publishing good quality content that earns links over time. Examples of black hat tactics would be purchasing links, building links in bulk with link submitter tools, creating blog networks just to build links to yourself, etc. Black hat methods don't have long lasting effects and are ultimately caught by search engines, and the sites are then penalized.

Avoiding Penalties

Read into Google's Webmaster Guidelines and follow them to prevent being hit by a penalty. The guidelines consist of basic rules such as avoiding writing low-quality content, avoiding publishing duplicate content, no thin content, no keyword stuffing and more.

How to Check if You've Been Hit by a Penalty

There are two types of penalties that can hit you: manual penalties or algorithmic penalties.

Manual penalties are penalties wherein a member of Google's webspam prevention department finds you breaking any of the Webmaster Guidelines and manually reports you in the system. You'll know if you've been hit by a manual penalty if you get a message in your Google Search Console account.

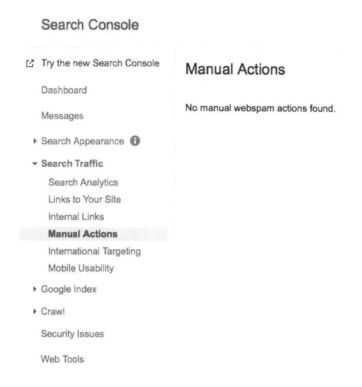

Algorithmic penalties, on the other hand, take place when Google updates the way websites are ranked, i.e., updates its algorithm. You'll know if you've been hit by a penalty if you experience a sudden drop in traffic and rankings. You can keep a check on your traffic using Google Analytics and check ranks using rank checker tools like SEMrush.

What to Do If Your Site Has Been Hit With a Penalty

If your site has been hit with a penalty, you have two choices: a disavow or a reconsideration. And choosing between them is based on what you've been penalized for.

A disavow can be used in the case your penalty is related to backlinks. Disavowing links does not remove the links, but it tells Google not to consider them when assessing your site. You can disavow your backlinks that are spammy and harming your sites ranking abilities.

A reconsideration request can be made in the case your site has been hit with a manual penalty. Through a reconsideration, you tell Google to look at your site after you've made actions to fix the problems stated in the manual action notification in Search Console.

Disavow Process

The following are the steps you need to follow to successfully go through the disavow process to inform Google which of your spammy backlinks not to consider:

1. Download a list of all of your backlinks using a backlink checker tool.
2. Sort through your backlinks and make a list of the low-quality spammy backlinks. These would be the links you built using black hat

techniques and low-quality backlinks with low trust scores.

3. Upload the list of links you want to be disavowed to the Google Disavow tool, which you can find at www.google.com/webmasters/tools/disavow-links-main. This document needs to be in .txt form, and the list of links to be disavowed needs to be in the format: domain:example.com. The list of links straight from the tool will probably be in the format such as http:// or www. To remove all of the HTTP and www's in bulk can use a free disavow generator tool to save time.

Reconsideration Process

Like mentioned above, reconsideration requests are only for manual penalties, a notification for which you receive in your Search Console account. Before you submit a reconsideration request, make sure you've made the changes required and fixed the issue the manual penalty was for. The notification should have all of the details of the issue.

When you're ready to submit the request, open your Search Console account and in the left-hand sidebar under 'search traffic' click 'manual actions'. Click on 'request a review' and upload your reconsideration request document. This document needs to be in .txt version and should be written in a format similar to an email or letter and contain information on the work carried out to fix the problem.

Start the document with an introduction to what the penalty was for and explain what's been done to fix it and provide proof as well. You won't be able to add any attachments so provide the proof by linking to a public Google sheet in Google Drive.

Remember that a real human from the Google webspam team will be reading this so keep the reconsideration document short.

SEO Checklists

On-Page SEO:

Insert your targeted keyword in the:

URL	
Article title	
Heading tags	
Content body	
Image title, alt tag, description	
Title tag	
Meta description	

Content Publishing Start to Finish:

Pre-Publication:

Keyword targeted article	
Optimize: • URL • Article title • Heading tags • Content body • Image title, alt tag, description • Title tag • Meta description	
Internal links with keyword rich anchor text	
Add any external links, if applicable	
Add call to action, if applicable	
Embed any assets you own, if applicable: video, map, widget, infographic, download, etc	

Post Publication:

Share across: • Facebook • Twitter • Google+ • Instagram • Pinterest	
Link to it internally	
Anchor text backlinks (quick wins like social bookmark, web 2.0)	

Updating Old Content:

Increase content length	
Update content to the latest version	
Embed any assets you own, if applicable: video, infographic, widget, download, etc	

Add an image if missing	
Add a call to action	
Edit and improve title tags and meta descriptions	
Further optimize on-page SEO elements if needed	

CTR Improvement:

Locate pages with low CTR rates in Search Console along with keywords they're ranking for	
Locate the keyword with the most impressions for each page	
Edit the title tags and meta description to make it more interesting and click-worthy, based on that keyword for each page	

individually
Wait two weeks and re-check CTR rates for each page individually.
Re-optimize and improve titles and meta descriptions for pages the CTR didn't improve.

Further Optimizing Pages Already Ranking:

Locate the keywords you're ranking for in your rank checker tool that are close to the #1 position, i.e., those with positions 2-20
Download lists of the keywords along with the URLs ranking for each
Further optimize each page for on-page SEO for the associated keyword
Create internal links to those URLs with the keywords as anchor text

Create backlinks (quick wins such as social bookmarks, web 2.0's) to those URLs with the keywords as anchor text

Keyword Research:

Make a list of 5-10 main seed keywords
Enter seed keywords into your keyword research tool of choice one by one
Download and combine lists of keywords generated from each seed keyword
Categorize keywords from the final list into keyword types: primary and secondary, service or product, location, evergreen, article, longtail, question, etc.
Prioritize their order based on competition and competitiveness levels

Create a content plan based on keyword chosen

Video Optimization:

Find keywords using the YouTube tab in Keywordtool.io
Input your keywords into the following: Video title Video description (add the main keyword a few times for good keyword density and add in your secondary keywords as well) Tags: Add your main keyword as well as all related keywords into the tags. Video thumbnail file image Video file name
Create a video timeline using timestamps.

Create closed captions and transcripts if necessary
Add videos to relevant playlists with each playlist having an SEO friendly title and description.
Interlink your videos to each other through cards and video displays at the end.

SEO Tasks:

Daily:	
Check Google Analytics for traffic stability	
Check Google Search Console for errors and messages	
Social signals for SEO through social media	
Weekly:	

Creating content based on keyword research	
Optimizing new content for on-page SEO before publishing	
Prospecting and outreach for link building	
Bi-weekly:	
Click-through-rate improvement	
Error fixing	
Request re-indexing in search console	
Check site speed	
Monthly:	
Order or build local citations	
Link building	
Update and improve old content	
Further optimizing pages ranking	
Reviews for local profiles	

Check ranks	
Every 6 months:	
Re-do and update keyword research	
Update your content plan based on keyword research	
One-time:	
Create and upload your sitemap to Search Console	
Create a robots.txt file if required	
Create profiles on local review platforms: Google My Business, Bing Places, Yelp, Yellow Pages	
Create any missing social platforms	

Further Your Learning!

If you'd like to take your learning further, I have an **SEO Course** for you which is available on my site at www.digiologist.com

SEO Course Details:

- Video tutorial format for hands on learning
- 4.5 Hours long
- 50+ video lessons

What the Course Covers:

- Ranking Factors Google Considers While Crawling Your Site
- How to Create Search Strings for Targeted Searches
- SEO Friendly Site Structure: Do's and Don'ts

- How to Create Sitemaps and Robots.txt files
- Finding Site Errors and How to Use Redirects
- Keyword Research Tutorial
- Optimizing On-Page SEO Elements
- Link Building Strategy Ideas
- Anchor Text Usage While Building Links
- Guest Posting Tutorial
- Unlinked Brand Mentions Tutorial
- Resource Link Building Tutorial
- Competitor Backlink Analysis Tutorial
- Internal Linking Tutorial
- Setting up Your Google My Business Page
- Citation Building Tutorial
- ...and More!

Course Feedback:

"Great course for beginners to intermediates SEOs. I've completed lots of SEO course's over the years,

but this course taught SEO in a unique way and managed to demonstrate areas in SEO that other courses are scared to touch."

"I loved this course because the instructor made everything easy to follow. The lessons were well made and I would recommend this course to anyone who wants to understand SEO. Just do it!"

"Great course. I learned a lot about on-page, off-page, keyword research. This course covers all SEO. Worth my time and investment."

"The instructor goes into great detail explaining all the details. The videos are great in both content and quality, and the format of the learning slides is a very sleek clean design. I would highly recommend this course to anybody wanting to learn some SEO."

Very informative course! One of the best SEO courses I've seen here. I love how it takes you from the extreme basics to more intermediate material very smoothly so anyone can take this course up. Highly recommend to anyone looking to build up their SEO skills beyond just the basics. ~ Student

"Fantastic quality course. It may be small but it is powerful. Thank you, Shivani. I highly recommend this course to anybody wanting to advance in SEO."

Course available at https://www.digiologist.com

Final Thoughts

Congratulations! You now have a better understanding of SEO and some strategies you can implement for your business. I hope this book helps you in building a stronger digital profile for your business.

If you enjoyed reading this book, please consider reviewing it on Amazon.

In case of any questions or feedback, you can email me at shivani@digiologist.com.

Thanks for reading!

Shivani Karwal

SEO Dictionary

0 – 9

301: The 301 redirection is used in moving a page permanently through permanent URL redirection from one URL to another URL. A 301 redirect means that the page has moved to a new location. So when the original URL is input in the browser or clicked on from an external location, the second page it was redirected to through the 301 opens instead of the original page.

302: The 302 redirect is a temporary redirection of one webpage to another, so it's used when the desired move of the page is only for some time till the final page move is being decided upon. It redirects users when they click on a link to another page instead for some time until the final destination is decided.

404: A 404 is an error code and is also known as a 'not found error' and occurs when a web page is not found. It is an error that is displayed when a user tries to open a webpage that no longer exists.

A

A/B Testing: Also known as 'split testing' involves performing two tests and comparing the results to see which option performed better and which to go with. The tests can be done by comparing two landing pages, two headings, two different titles, different content bodies, emails subject lines, etc.

Above the Fold: Refers to the top half of a webpage that is visible to the user without scrolling down. The 'above the fold' section of a page is an important section as it is what users see without scrolling, so it needs to contain important information and be exciting to make the user want to scroll down as well.

Absolute Link: An absolute link is a link that contains the full URL of the page including the domain and the file name for the page after the slash (link to a particular page other than the homepage) if it is to a deeper page. An absolute link is different from a relative link as a relative link doesn't contain the domain and links to a particular file and can be opened only from within the document it is contained in and related to. An absolute link can be opened from anywhere.

For example:

Absolute Link: http://www.site.com/about.html
Relative Link: /about.html

Age: In SEO, age refers to site age, i.e., domain age. The older a domain, the more trustworthy it is to Google. This is only one of the many factors looked at by Google though. A site with an older domain age can be seen as a site the webmaster thought was worth renewing each time its expiration date neared, thereby having some value worth renewing.

Algorithm: In terms of SEO, it refers to Google's ranking algorithm i.e., the process of determining which sites will rank at what position as a result when a query is searched.

Algorithmic Rate: The rate at which changes are made to Google's search algorithm, i.e., the changes made to Google's rules and process for deciding which sites to rank and their ranking position assignment. Google changes its algorithm frequently to better results.

Alias: An online persona created for outreach purposes, especially for link building. This is done to either hide one's identity for professional or personal reasons or to communicate and fit in better with audiences or prospective linkers.

Alt Attribute: The alt attribute specifies the alt text for an image to provide alternative information that describes what the image is about in the case that the user cannot view the image or it is unable to load properly due to an error or not fast enough due to slow page load speed.

Alt Tag: Alt tag is a common shorthand term that refers to alt attribute. See alt attribute above.

Alt Text: The alt text refers to the words/text that make up the alt tag or alt attribute. Alt attribute, alt tag, and alt text are the same.

Analytics: Analytics in SEO usually refers to Google Analytics, which is the most widely used tool to measure a site's analytics.

Anchor Text: Anchor text refers to the text that makes up a link. It is the word or group of words that are linkable and is the text that can be clicked on when opening a link. It is important for SEO as it describes what the link is about to search engines.

AND Modifier: The 'AND' modifier is a search modifier/operator that can be used to perform a more detailed Google search wherein you can search two queries at once and ensure they both show up in search results.

Article Spinning: An article spinner is a software that uses an existing article and converts it into a unique article by replacing words, re-phrasing, and re-writing. Article spinning is used for link building purposes when content pieces are needed to be posted to article directories and web 2.0 sites.

Audit: An SEO audit is done to perform an in-depth analysis of a website to find errors and improvement areas to make the site more SEO friendly. Some areas audits look into are: numbers, nature, and quality of backlinks, missing or duplicate title tags, headers, alt tags, site structure, duplicate content, etc.

Authority: Authority metrics such as domain authority, page authority, etc. measure how likely a site or a page is to rank in search engines.

B

Backlink: Backlinks are incoming links to your site from external sites pointing to your site.

Backlink Profile: A sites backlink profile is the portfolio of all links that are currently linking to it from external sites. Some factors to study in a backlink profile are number, quality, and relevancy of links.

Backlink Profile Density: Refers to the density of the anchor text in a sites backlinks, i.e., the percent of backlinks with the main keyword used as the anchor text. This refers to exact match anchor text usage, and it is advised to keep it around 10% as over-usage of exact match keywords as anchor text will get a site penalized.

Bad Neighborhood: A bad neighborhood refers to websites that have been penalized by search engines and seen as participating in spammy activities such as poor content, over usage of ads, spammy links, blackhat activities.

Bait and Switch: Involves advertising your product at a low price but making it unavailable or out of stock when the customer goes to buy it and then to try to sell them something else instead.

Below the Fold: Refers to the bottom half of a webpage that is visible only when the user scrolls down and not immediately visible when a webpage is opened.

Black Hat SEO: All activities that violate search engine guidelines by partaking aggressive techniques that concentrate more on ranking in the SERPs rather than providing value to the reader.

Blacklisted: Sites that have been de-indexed by search engines due to spammy practices and no longer appear in search results.

Blended Search: Through blended search, search engines aim to provide users the most relevant results from a variety of courses and through a variety of formats such as news, local results, images, videos, etc. instead of just text.

Bookmark: Web pages bookmarked on social bookmarking sites, which search engines see as quality content and a backlink.

Boolean Operator: Boolean operators are words that act as modifiers to improve and conduct more detailed searches. Some examples of operators/modifiers are the AND, OR, - commands.

Boolean Searching: Using Boolean operators a.k.a search modifiers to conduct more detailed and specific searches to have a greater chance of finding exactly what the user is searching for.

Bot: Bots or robots or web crawlers or spiders, browse the web to index pages to rank in search results.

Bounce Rate: The percentage of one page only visits to your site by users where users click off of the site after viewing only one page.

Brand Mentions: Mentions of your brand online on external sites. These may be 'unlinked brand mentions' in some cases where your brand is mentioned but a link back to your site is not provided which leads to a link building opportunity.

Brand Stacking: Refers to multiple page one rankings from the same domain for brand related searches.

Branded Keywords: Keywords containing the brand name or company name or variation of the brand or company name used to search for that particular brand or company.

Branded Link: A link with the brand name as the anchor text.

Branded Search: Search conducted using branded keywords.

Breadcrumbs: Links that show the user the path they've taken to reach a specific page on your site, their current location, how one page relates to another and the path back to the homepage.

Broad Match: Partial matches of your main keywords as anchor text. Involves using different variations of your main anchor text by either partially using words from your main keyphrases or combining the main keyword with other words to create partial match anchor text, i.e., broad match anchor text.

Broken Link: A link to a 404 page, i.e., to a page with a 'not found' error due to the page being removed or never existing in the first place (incorrect URL).

Broken Link Building: Involves using a tool to scale finding outgoing broken links from sites in your niche and emailing the webmaster to let them know the existence of such a broken link and requesting them to replace the link with a link to your site instead.

C

Cache: Google cache refers to snapshots or copies of web pages taken by Google while indexing sites to serve as backups in cases where the page is temporarily unavailable in the future.

Canonical Tag: Helps webmasters prevent duplicate content issues as it allows telling search engines which page is the preferred page for that content or the original page for that content, so search engines know which version to show.

Canonical URL: The preferred URL for the same content used on various pages indicated by the use of a canonical tag.

Canonicalization: A web page that can be loaded using different URLs. For example:

http://www.example.com

http://www.example.com/index.html

http://example.com

ccTLD: Country specific TLDs (top level domains) such as .ca, .co.uk, .in, .au etc.

Churn: The rate at which links on a webpage are changed over time either by removal or replacement.

Citation: An online reference and display of your company name, address and phone number (NAP) in that particular order. Similar to link building, citations should be placed across various external sites for improving local rankings.

Citation Flow: A site metric between 0 to 100 indicating how powerful a URL may be based on the number and quality of links pointing to it.

Click Bait: Click bait is content whose main purpose is to encourage and increase clicks on it by users through catchy headlines. These headlines may be clever and catchy but may also be negatively viewed if they're misleading, fake or distracting.

Cloaking: Serving search engines and your users different content for a web page by misleading search engines about the content on a webpage.

CMS: Content management systems are frameworks that design and develop a site's content. They're used to publish, edit and display a site's content.

Code Swapping: Involves optimizing a page for high rankings in SERPs and then using a different page in its place once it starts to rank.

Competitor Analysis: An analysis of your competitors SEO efforts by using SEO tools to check keywords they're using, keywords they're ranking for, plugins they're using, their site structure, an analysis of their incoming backlinks and link building tactics, etc.

Conceptual Link: Links that search engines attempt to understand beyond just their anchor text by looking at the words surrounding the link.

Content Calendar: A content plan including which topics will be covered and go live on a site and on which days with the topics being based on keyword research.

Content Curation: A content curator is involved with the research, organization, writing, and publishing of content online.

Content Farm: Websites that contain a large amount of low-quality content published with the aim of ranking.

Content Gaps: Topics in your niche that are not covered enough or at all and that are great opportunities to address and fill the void.

Content Mill: A company that hires numerous writers to write content for its customers. They're a place for digital marketers or businesses to find freelance writers to outsource their content to.

Content Syndication: Involves posting your content onto third-party sites for more exposure.

Contextual Link: A link found in a body of content surrounded by text instead of just a stand-alone link.

Conversion: When a site visitor converts into a sale or takes a desired action such as completing a download or filling a form.

Conversion Rate: The rate at which site visitors convert into sales or take a desired action.

Conversion Rate Optimization: Optimizing, i.e., bettering or improving the conversion rate.

Crawl: Browsing of your site by search engine robots to index pages.

Crawl Depth: The extent to which search engines crawl a website and how deep and far they go into a site from the home page.

Crawl Frequency: How often search engine robots crawl a website.

Crawler: Bots or robots or web crawlers or spiders, browse the web to index pages to rank in search results.

CSS: Stands for Cascading style sheets and allows for changing the style of a webpage by adding fonts, colors, etc.

CTA: Stands for call to action and is an instruction to site visitors based on the desired action a webmaster wants them to take such as completing a sale, downloading a piece of content, filling a form, etc.

D

De-indexed: A site that has been de-listed, i.e., removed from search engine results due to spammy practices.

Dead Link: A link that no longer exists due to removal.

Deep Link: An internal link that is reached by navigating far from the home page.

Delinking: Unlinking, i.e., removing a link to a site.

Delisting: A site that has been de-indexed, i.e., removed from search engine results due to spammy practices.

Direct Traffic: Traffic from visitors that reach your site directly without a source or referral but instead by typing your site address into the address bar.

Directory: A site containing lists of businesses.

Disallow: A command that can be inserted in the robotts.txt file of a site to disallow, i.e., hide pages from search engines to prevent them from being indexed and ranked.

Disavow: Disavowing links is a process using the Google disavow tool that allows publishers to tell Google which incoming links to their site they don't want to be associated with their site and be considered while looking at the sites backlink profile.

DNS: An Internet system that translates a domain name into an IP address.

Do-follow: A link with a do-follow status passes link juice and is visible to search engines. Also see no-follow.

Domain: A name for a website that makes it easy to access by acting like an address that can be entered into the browser to access a site.

Domain Authority: A site authority metric from 0 to 100 that measures the power of a domain and how likely it is to rank in search engines.

Doorway Farm: Sites with low-quality pages that are optimized to rank well for particular terms but act as a door or bridge with the purpose of sending visitors to a different page.

Doorway Page: Low-quality pages that are optimized to rank well for a particular term but act as a door or bridge as they send visitors to a different page.

Duplicate Content: Content that has already been published on the web. This may be content a site owner owns but just publishes to a few different pages or content that a second person steals from a site to post it on their own.

Dwell Time: The time a visitor spends on your site before returning to the search results page.

Dynamic URL: A URL created as a result of a specific search.

E

Earned Link: A link that is not built and one that is obtained without any effort when a site naturally links to another site without requesting a link.

Editorial Link: A contextual link, i.e., a link found in a body of content surrounded by text instead of just a stand-alone link.

Entry Page: The first page of your site that a visitor sees when they open your site, i.e., the page the visitors enter your site from.

Ethical SEO: SEO that is done using non-spammy techniques that comply with search engine guidelines.

Evergreen Content: Content that is not seasonal and that will always be searched for.

Exact Match Domain: A domain containing an exact match of the main keyword or keyphrase a site wants to rank for.

Exact Match Anchor Text: Anchor text containing an exact match of the main keyword or keyphrase a site wants to rank for.

Exit Page: The page a user last visits on your site, i.e., the page from which the user exits your site.

Exit Rate: The rate of visitors that exit out of your website from a page beyond the home-page in a session.

Expired Domain: A domain that was not renewed for hosting and has now expired and is available for purchase.

External Link: A link from an external site pointing to your site, i.e., an incoming link.

F

Forums: Discussion boards across the web for various topics and niches.

Fragment URL: A URL containing a fragment identifier, i.e., the part of a URL after the # that is the optional last part of the link.

Fuzzy Search: A fuzzy search finds matches even when the user misspells the search query or only enters partial words.

G

Gateway Page: Standalone pages that are highly optimized for a keyword and are built with the aim of ranking fast for that keyword. These are often low in quality and sometimes even computer generated.

Generic Anchor Text: Anchor text that does not contain keywords and is general and mostly directional such as 'site', 'here', 'click here' etc.

Geo-keywords: Keywords with a location modifier and local intent attached such as 'Toronto restaurants' instead of just 'restaurants'.

Google Analytics: An analytics software by Google that provides a significant amount of data related to your sites such as visitors, page views, the location of users, devices users used to access your site and much more.

Google Bowling: Manipulating external factors to penalize and de-rank your competitor sites.

Google Webmaster Tools: A software by Google to keep a check on the overall health of your site and detect any errors or penalties.

Google Bot: Google's web crawler that crawls web pages for indexing purposes.

Grey Hat SEO: SEO techniques that are not as ethical as white hat but not as risky and spammy as black hat and may or may not result in a site being de-indexed.

Guest Posting: Posting content written by you on external blogs to gain exposure for your site by appearing in front of other sites audiences by writing for them.

H

H1 Tag: The header 1 tag on a webpage used for the first heading of the page.

Heading Tag: Tags used any of a webpages headings from H1 to H5.

Heatmap: A software that shows what users want when they visit your website, what they're looking at and their behavior and navigation pattern.

Hidden Text: A black hat technique involving changing the color the font of some parts of keyword heavy text to match the background to hide it from visitors.

Hits: Refers to page hits when a webpage on a site is opened.

Hotlinking: A form of bandwidth theft by adding another sites media such as images and videos directly onto your site in a way that they appear on your site instead of directly adding them to your site. They are displayed using the other sites server and therefore use up their bandwidth.

HTML Sitemap: A sitemap created for users to allow them to navigate your site better. Also, see XML sitemap.

Hummingbird: A Google algorithm that came out in 2013 that started taking into consideration the entire search query, i.e., each word of the search query to understand user intent better.

Hyperlink: A clickable link.

I

Impression: A page impression is generated each time a page on a site is viewed.

Inbound Link: An external link, i.e., an incoming link from an external site pointing to your site.

Index: A search engines database that contains a compilation of all information gathered when crawling websites.

Interlinking: Linking from your site to other pages on your site, i.e., internal links.

Internal Linking: See interlinking.

Intitle: Modifier: A search operator used in conducting Boolean searches to find text in page titles across the web.

Inurl: Modifier: A search operator used in conducting Boolean searches to find text in URLs across the web.

K

Keyword: The search terms users insert in search engines to find what they're looking for.

Keyword Cannibalization: Occurs when the same keyword is used in and targeted by multiple pages on a site.

Keyword Density: The percentage of a keyword being present in a post. Can be calculated by: (number of times keyword is present in the article/total number of words in the article) x 100

Keyword Funnel: Keyword funnels track the relationship between and categorize different sets of keywords.

Keyword Proximity: The distance between search-phrases words to each other in the case they're not written in the same order and exactly like the search phrase.

Keyword Research: Research conducted to find relevant high traffic keywords to target on a site.

Keyword Stuffing: Spammy over-usage of keywords on a web page.

L

Landing Page: The page users land on when users click on a search engine result.

Link Acquisition: The process of acquiring backlinks to your site either by building or earning links.

Link Bait: High-quality link-worthy content that is created with the aim of earning backlinks.

Link Building: Process of building external links pointing to your site either manually by link submission through account creation or by requesting external site owners to do so.

Link Churn: The rate at which links on a webpage are changed over time either by removal or replacement.

Link Decay: When your backlinks either lose value over time or decrease in number.

Link Density: Refers to the number of links on a page whether outgoing or incoming. A page with many outgoing links will have a high link density and vice versa.

Link Earning: Earning links naturally without any effort instead of building them, i.e., when a site naturally links to another site without requesting a link.

Link Equity: The influence that incoming links have on a page's ability to rank.

Link Exchange: Exchange of links between two parties where both link to each other and gain reciprocal links.

Link Farm: A set of web pages or websites created to link to a particular page with the aim of ranking that page.

Link Hoarding: The practice of refraining from linking to any external sites to prevent the transfer of link juice.

Link Juice: The 'power' or 'authority' passed when a site links to another site.

Link Laundering: Involves pointing a large number of low-quality tier 3 links to the second tier sites which point to links to your main site.

Link Pathway: The path users use to get from one webpage to another.

Link Poaching: Stealing your competitor's backlinks by having the original sites replace them with links to your site.

Link Popularity: Number of backlinks that point to a site.

Link Profile: The portfolio of all incoming links to a website. Factors like the number of links, quality, relevancy, follow status' etc. make up a link profile.

Link Pyramid: A tiered link building approach wherein set of tier 1 or 'base links' point to the main site, a set of tier 2 or middle links point to the tier 1 links and a set of tier 3 links which are usually lower in quality but high in number, point to the tier 2 links.

Link Reclamation: Getting back lost links that were once pointing to your site.

Link Rot: The rate at which a site loses links in numbers or the current links lose value.

Link Velocity: Rate at which a site acquires backlinks.

Link Wheel: A group of sites that strategically link to each other. For example, in the case of 6 sites, namely. A, B, C, D, E and F. With A being the main site, then B links to C, C links to D, D links to E, E links to F, F links to B and B links to A, thereby completing the wheel.

Link: Modifier: A search operator used in conducting Boolean searches to find all pages linking to a certain site, i.e., the backlinks.

Local Search: Allows users to search for geographic specific searches and get back results based on their location and the use of location modifiers used in their search query.

Local SEO: SEO practices that aim to rank a site in local search based on the location the search is made in and for local queries.

Localization: The translation of a webpage for a different culture or language.

Location Modifier: Location-based words used to make the search query location specific. For example, the search query 'Toronto restaurants' would have a location modifier being present in it rather than the search 'restaurant'.

Longtail: Longer and more descriptive keyphrases that search for something specific and more detailed.

M

Mail Merge: An automated email campaign sent to a list of recipients but still being slightly customized by pulling variants from the list such as name, site, etc. for each email sent.

Manual Penalty: The negative impact to a websites ranks based on an algorithm released by Google or as a result of a manual review.

Meta Description: A short snippet or summary that summarizes the content of a web page and is shown in search engine results.

Meta Keywords: A list of keywords or tags that tell search engines what the page is about. They're a list of tags in the form of words or key phrases. They've been said to be a waste of time as Google doesn't consider them, but other search engines still do.

Meta Tags: Meta tag description. See meta description.

Metadata: Refers to the meta title (or title tag) and meta description.

Metric: Scores such as domain authority, page authority, etc. that define an overall site, a domain or pages power and ability to rank well.

Mini Site: A site with a keyword rich domain linking to the main site and created to rank in search engines along with the mini-site to capture multiple top spots in the SERPs.

Minus Modifier: A search operator used in conducting Boolean searches to subtract or eliminate a word from search results.

Mirror Site: Exact copies of your main site that are created to rank for terms and redirect to the main site once they start ranking.

Modifier: A search operator that is used to modify and refine search results by making it more detailed.

Money Site: Your main site which links are built to and all SEO efforts are done for.

N

Naked Link: A link that is just a URL without any anchor text.

NAP: Name, address and phone number of a website which makes up its citation.

NAP Consistency: Ensuring all NAP references on the web for your business are exactly the same information in the same format.

Natural Link: A link naturally earned and not built.

Navigation: The framework, organization, and navigation structure of a site.

Negative SEO: Using external factors and efforts to negatively impact a competitor site so it loses rankings.

Niche: A specific topic or category.

No-follow: Links that don't have a do-follow status. They don't pass link juice and aren't visible to search engines.

No-index: The no-index code is used on a page to tell search engines not to index the page and not show it in search results.

Not Found Error: A 404 error when a webpage is not found due to being deleted or the page URL never existing in the first place.

O

Off-Page: SEO efforts taking place off the main site and through external sites.

On-Page: SEO efforts taking place on the main site itself.

One Way Link: A link that a site points to another site without the second site pointing a link back to the original site.

Operator: A search modifier that is used to modify and refine search results by making it more detailed.

OR Modifier: A search operator used in conducting Boolean searches to search for either of two key phrases or keywords.

Organic Link: A link that is naturally earned and not built.

Organic Search Results: Unpaid search results where sites rank in search engines as a result of SEO efforts instead of payment through ads.

Organic SEO: Process of ranking a site in search engines organically without purchasing search engine ads.

Organic Traffic: All traffic coming from clicks on pages ranking in search engines organically.

ORM: Online reputation management which involves having a good clean online image where only positive pages show up while searching for a person, company or brands name.

Outbound Link: Links on your site pointing to external sites.

P

Page Title: Contains the title of the webpage that explains what the webpage is about. It should be optimized and contain keywords.

Pagerank: An old concept that used to measure the power and authority of web pages. Pagerank is no longer updated and so, outdated.

Pageviews: When a user visits a page on a website it is counted as a pageview.

Pagination: Involves spreading the content of an article onto multiple pages instead of just one single page. This can be done by having a 'next' option on each page to click on to view the next part of the article.

Paid Link: A sponsored link that is built after payment to the site owner.

Palindromic SEO: Involves SEO activities that target queries in reverse order as well. Palindromes are words which when read forward and backward have the same meaning.

Panda: A Google algorithm released in 2011 to lower the rank of poor quality thin content.

Parasite SEO: Involves building pages with your content on external high authority sites to make ranking content easier.

PBN: Private blog network. Creating a set of sites solely to link to your main site.

Penalty: The negative impact on a site's rankings due to an update in Google's ranking algorithm.

Penguin: A Google algorithm update released in 2012 to penalize sites spamming search engines with low quality 'thin' content. It aimed to return high-quality results at the top.

Permalink: A permanent link i.e., static hyperlink.

Persona: In terms of link building, a persona is an online alias created for outreach purposes, especially for link building. This is done to either hide one's identity for professional or personal reasons or to communicate and fit in better with audiences or prospective linkers.

Personalized Search: Personalized search results that are relevant to one's preferences and are delivered based on one's search history through browser cookie records.

Phantom Page: A webpage that is optimized for search engines rather than humans.

Phantom Update: An unconfirmed Google algorithm update that was a quality update leading to the filtering out of low-quality content with low ranks.

Pigeon: A Google algorithm update released in 2014 aiming to increase the rank and number of local results in the SERPs.

Pillow Links: Links with diverse anchor text such as branded anchors, miscellaneous anchors, naked links, etc. These are created to dilute the use of the main keywords as anchor text as over-usage of those can lead to a penalty. This is done for anchor text ratio correction.

Ping: Pinging Google is like URL submission. It allows you to let Google know about a newly added page or site update yourself rather than waiting for Google to find out while indexing your site next.

Position: The rank number of a page in the SERPs.

Poison Word: Words that will decrease your ranking if found in your site content.

Q

Query: A search query, i.e., the keyword or keyphrase entered in a search engine.

Quotation Mark Modifier: A search operator used in conducting Boolean searches to search for an exact word or words in content based on the format placed within the quotation marks.

R

Rank: The position a webpage has for a keyword search in the SERPs.

Reciprocal Links: Two-way links where both sites link to each other.

Reclamation: Having lost or removed links reclaimed by having them added again.

Reconsideration Request: A request to have Google review your site after you've completed and fixed the issues on your site related to the manual penalty your site received.

Redirect: Moving one URL to another, i.e., having a different URL open instead of the one originally entered in the browser.

Referral Traffic: Traffic to your site from mentions of your site on external websites.

Reinclusion: A request to Google to remove the penalty to your site and re-include you in search engines and restore rankings.

Related: Modifier: A search operator used in conducting Boolean searches to find related sites.

Relative Link: A link that works within a document to point to parts in the document and doesn't require the use of the full URL but only the part after .com. Relative links don't work outside of the document they're intended for.

Reputation Management: Online reputation management which involves having a good clean online image where only positive pages show up while searching for a person, company or brands name

Resource Page: Web pages that contain a list of related resource pages on a particular topic.

Reverse Image Search: Searching using an image instead of text to find the original use of the image and all other sources where it has been used.

Rich Snippets: The extra text that shows up in search results under a sites meta description for more details. These are links to important pages on the site such as the about page, services page, contact page, etc.

Robots.txt: A file uploaded to a site that informs search crawlers which web pages to not crawl on the site and not include in search results.

Roundup: A roundup article involves reaching out to experts for their opinions on a topic or question and compiling it all into an article.

S

Sandbox: A temporary filtering of new websites for some time by Google before they're live and ranked in the SERPs.

Schema Markup: A type of data that makes it easier for search engines to browse, sort through and interpret the information in your site and provide the most relevant search results to users.

Scrape: Refers to data scraping, i.e., collecting and compiling data.

Search Operators: A search modifier that is used to modify and refine search results by making it more detailed.

Search Query: The keyword or keyphrase entered in search engines.

Search Strings: A combination of keywords and search operators used to conduct a refined search.

Search Term: See search query.

SERP: Search engine results page.

Shallow Content: Thin low-quality content.

Site Structure: The organizational structure a site uses to present its pages and content.

Sitemap: Can be of two types: HTML sitemap, XML sitemap, where an HTML sitemap is an organizational representation of a site's content and made for users to easily navigate site content, and an XML sitemap is made for search crawlers to navigate the site easily.

SLD: Stands for second level domain and is basically the domain name. For example, in example.com, example is the SLD and .com is the TLD (top level domain).

Spider: Bots or robots or web crawlers or spiders that browse the web to index pages to rank in search results.

Spinning: An article spinner is a software that uses an existing article and converts it into a unique article by replacing words, re-phrasing, and re-writing. Article spinning is used for link building purposes when numerous content pieces are needed to be posted to article directories and web 2.0 sites.

Split Testing: Also known as 'a/b testing' involves performing two tests and comparing the results to see which option performed better and which to go with. The tests can be done by comparing two landing pages, two headings, two different titles, different content bodies, emails subject lines, etc

Static URL: A URL whose link stays the same no matter how the input or where it is opened from.

Static Website: A website displayed to the user exactly as stored and not changed.

Stop Word: Words ignored by search engines to speed up search result delivery. Stop words are common words that don't have much meaning such as is, an, the, etc.

Strings: A combination of keywords and search operators used to conduct a refined search.

Subdirectory: A subdirectory is like a folder that is part of your site and your domain and takes the format: example.com/subdomain and is used to create a separate area on your site for specific content or a specific purpose. Unlike a subdomain, a subdirectory is considered part of the main site and reaps all benefits of the main site such as backlinks and authority of the main site.

Subdomain: A domain that is part of a larger domain and takes the format: subdomain.example.com. It is used to create a separate area on your site for specific content or a specific purpose and is considered a separate domain by Google.

Subtract Modifier: The subtract modifier is a search modifier/operator that can be used remove specific words from Google search results to make your search more detailed.

Syndication: Involves posting your content onto third-party sites for more exposure.

T

Tags: Tags in SEO refer to title tags, meta tags, header tags, alt tags.

Thin Content: Low-quality shallow content.

Three Way Linking: A linking structure in which three parties decide to link to one another in the format: site A links to site B, site B links to site C and site C links to site A.

Tier 1: The high-quality first level links in a tiered link structure that point to your main site.

Tier 2: The second level of links in a tiered link building structure that are built to point to the tier

1 links. They are lesser quality than the tier 1 links but not bad quality. Usually built using web 2.0 sites, through article submissions, etc.

Tier 3: The third level of links in a tiered link building structure that are built to point to the tier 2 links. They are the lowest in quality and are built in large numbers and built using tools.

Tiered Link Building: A link building structure in which 3 level of links are built, namely tiers 1, 2 and 3. Tier 1 links link to the main site, tier 2 links link to the tier 1 links and tier 3 links link to the tier 2 links.

Title Tag: The title assigned to a webpage that appears in search results.

TLD: Top-level domain. It is the part of the site URL that comes after the domain name. Some examples of TLDs are: .com. .org, .co, .edu etc.

Trackback: When site A links to site B and site A automatically gets a trackback link from site B as the author of site B set up automatic notifications and the giving out such trackback links when a site links to it.

Transactional Keywords: Keyphrases with an intent to purchase. For example, 'buy laptop', 'house for sale' etc.

Transcribe: Having the audio of a video translated to text so it can be used as an article as well.

Trust flow: A score between 0 to 100 predicting how trustworthy a site is.

Two Way Link: See reciprocal link.

U

Unethical SEO: Includes all SEO practices that are spammy and don't comply with search engine guidelines.

Universal Search: Blended search results containing a mixture of media as results such as articles, videos, news, images, etc.

Unlinked Brand Mentions: Web pages that mention your brand but don't link back.

Unnatural Link: A link that is built through efforts and not naturally earned.

V

Vanity URL: A customized and usually shortened URL that is branded or contains the topic in the URL for presentation purposes instead of a long messy link.

Vertical Search: A topical search that searches for a specific topic or a search for a particular format of content.

W

Web 2.0: Websites with user-generated content that allow anyone to register, create and publish content.

Webmaster: The person in charge of making site changes, corrections, additions and overall site maintenance.

Webmaster Tools: A software by Google to keep a check on the overall health of your site and detect any errors or penalties.

White Hat SEO: Non-spammy SEO tactics that comply with search engine guidelines.

Whois: Domain registration info that displays information such as domain owner name, phone number, address, etc.

X

XML Sitemap: A sitemap created for search crawlers to easily navigate the site.

Notes:

Notes:

Notes:

Notes:

Notes:

Notes:

Notes:

Printed in Great Britain
by Amazon